LEAP!

On Faith, Doubt, and the Community Beside Your Flight

Colin Holba

StreamLineBooks.co

STREAMLINE

Copyright © 2021 Colin Holba

All rights reserved

No part of this book may be reproduced, or stored in a retrieval system, or transmitted in any form or by any means, electronic, mechanical, photocopying, recording, or otherwise, without express written permission of the publisher.

ISBN-13: 9798533298575
ISBN-10: 1477123456

Cover design by: Will Severns | QwillCreative.com
Cover photo: Unsplash | @vherliann
Library of Congress Control Number: 2018675309
Printed in the United States of America

"Always pass on what you have learned." —Yoda

I'm dedicating this book to my little one.

We don't know what your face looks like or what you'll accomplish in life. As I write this, we haven't even heard your heartbeat yet, but your existence has changed my perception of the world.

Your little life has changed how I see everything—from your beautiful mother, to work, to finances, to what I'm passionate about, and to the pursuit of wisdom in Christ.

Most importantly, you have changed the way I pray.

FOREWORD

I knew it was a God thing when Colin reached out and asked me to write the foreword for his book. Honored was my first reaction, followed by a million ideas of what I could say. Then, I was humbled by an overwhelming sense of just how powerful our God is.

Colin and I met at a very interesting crossroads in life. It was in my fifth year in the NFL. I was in a groove in my career, with supreme confidence in my ability to do my job at the highest level. However, during the second week of training camp, as I was running down field during a drill I tore my ACL. A total freak incident with no contact. Even today, I don't understand the cause. But in an instant, I was out for the season.

Colin was in his rookie year and had just been cut by the Pittsburgh Steelers. So, the Jacksonville Jaguars brought Colin in to replace me for the season. Fresh out of college and hungry to play in the NFL, Colin walked in and I taught him everything I could about long snapping. He did a fantastic job. He even won a couple of playoff games—something I have yet to achieve in my career. One of those playoff wins came against none other than the Pittsburgh Steelers.

There's a common saying in the NFL:

"Football is what you do, it's not who you are."

I had to learn this the hard way when I tore my ACL. I have played football since I was in the fifth grade. Suddenly, I was no longer a football player, and had no idea who I was. Colin will tell you that he has also learned this lesson in his own way.

There's a side to the NFL that the average fan doesn't know: the waiver wire and the "journeymen" that live it. It's a lifestyle for a constantly churning 40% of NFL players. Most of these men are just numbers to most who often forget that these players are people. People with families, hopes, aspirations, and stories to tell.

Seeing a friend, a hardworking coworker, a mentor, or your wife's best friend's husband get cut never gets easy, but always leads to great locker-room conversation. My favorite piece of wisdom given to me when I was a young player was a little locker-room sermon on Jeremiah 29:11.

God has a purpose and a plan for everyone, to prosper, not to harm. If you believe in God, why would you not believe that He has an amazing plan for you? Even if you just lost your job by tearing your ACL and had to teach some stranger named Colin Holba how to replace you.

God created a galaxy with more than 300 trillion suns (WISE J224607). So why would you ever put a limit on or try to define what He has called you to do? He is LIMITLESS. If He created everything we have ever known, then He can surely take a kid that has been cut once or twice and use him for His glory. In the NFL, or anywhere on the planet.

Believe that God has a plan for you. A BIG and BOLD plan, full of unimaginable things. Believe it! No matter where you are in life you can be assured that you are in the exact spot meant for you because it is God's plan for you.

Colin is able to speak about how to trust God in the middle of uncertainty as well as anyone. His life exemplifies time and time again how God can use anyone anywhere for good, regardless of the circumstance. From football, to baseball, to substitute teaching, back to football, and bouncing from team-to-team living the "journeyman" lifestyle. It's amazing to see the environments where God has placed Colin, and how well God prepared him each time before he arrived.

Four years later, Colin and I are still playing football, but we know it isn't who we are. Sure, we are very passionate about football, long snapping specifically; but it isn't our purpose. Football is merely a platform for God to use us. That's the purpose.

Colin has done an outstanding job on this book. I hope it speaks to you wherever you are in life, and encourages you to find your purpose and take the Leap!

Carson Tinker

INTRODUCTION

"Never be afraid to trust an unknown future to a known God." —Corrie ten Boom

Oftentimes, I am scared to pray this honest prayer:

"Lord, use me in the manner in which you see most fit. Lord guide me, open my eyes to see your path, soften my anxiety of control, and release it to the utmost trust I can possibly have. Lord, use me however you see fit to advance your Kingdom."

That prayer, even to write it out, gives chills down my neck and makes my skin tingle. It is a prayer of submission, but most importantly a prayer of childlike trust. As we grow up, we become more dependent on ourselves. The old adage says, "If you want something done right, you have to do it yourself," and is a statement riddled with control and self-reliance. There is a sense of pride, when we are children, to show off for our parents, teachers, and friends—to show them we can do something on our own. We show them we can tie our own shoes, make our own sandwiches, and even make our own money.

Those things are not bad—they show development and growth.

Somewhere along the line, we become overly dependent on ourselves. That sense of independence can turn into a slippery slope of self-reliance.

If there's one thing I've learned through an unpredictable career in sports, marriage while out on the road, and preparing to raise a child . . . it is that we *need* community. We need God for direction. We need friends, parents, siblings, and therapy dogs. We need people to assist our loved ones when we can't, and mentors to pour into us when we are empty and have nothing to offer.

Additionally, we are called to serve others in the same way. To love without condition and show grace in the process.

"Take delight in the LORD, and he will give you the desires of your heart." —Psalm 37:4

During my freshman year of college, I turned that verse into a daily prayer—when I wanted to walk onto the University of Louisville's (UofL) football team. It was a prayer of selfishness— a prayer about me and my little kingdom. That verse, through wisdom and context, reveals a different desire: the more we delight in the Lord, *the more our desires become His desires.*

We long for selfish paths to be made known and secured, but instead of a self-centered prayer, consider this:

"Lord, use me however you see fit to advance your Kingdom, because *that* is the desire of my heart."

Between Psalm 37:4 and consistent prayer, God is using us in his way. Through this we receive a new barometer for emotional health and well-being.

So to adjust the mindset of my original "Dedication."

My child, as your father, I pray to model God's desire for you from the moment you are born.

You are an inspiration, and my hope for you and any other individual who read this book is this: that you would realize there is no such thing as a "Leap of faith." Instead, take a step back from your lofty goals and drop to your knees. Pray not that *your* will be done, but God's—in a similar manner to how Jesus prayed on a regular basis.

Sometimes we just need a little nudge in that direction. My hope is that this book nudges you toward deeper prayer and relationship with God. And in the process of humbling yourself to both knees, you would learn to Leap with both feet.

LEAP!

By Colin Holba

PART 1

CHAPTER 1

"'It certainly is a puzzle.' He turned back to the broken road. 'But sometimes to find the answer, you have to take a leap of faith.'" —Dianna Hardy, Summers End

In my earliest days of childhood, there was really only one thing I adamantly prayed for. It was a vain prayer, but simply something I wanted to achieve.

I prayed every single night as a child to one day become a college athlete.

Around that time, in middle school, I played both baseball and football. People would ask "Colin, if you had to choose, which sport would you prefer if you could only play one?"

As a teenager, there was no distinction for me. Both sports were so unique—the people I played with as well as the physical and mental preparation that went into both. The skill sets each game required were so different and had their own ways of drawing me in.

Even in high school, I was never asked by any of my coaches to choose one over the other. It wasn't until my junior year in high school, when on my own merit, I chose baseball. It wasn't that I didn't like football anymore—to me it was just a future-oriented decision. In hindsight, it was probably the first time I "took control" from God in my own life. I had prayed and prayed to be a college athlete, so it was time for me to lock it in, focus on one sport and attain that dream. After one year of varsity football as a long snapper and third string QB, I hung up my pads and decided baseball was the sport for me.

Zero regrets about that decision.

My senior year, I went to all the football games I could, cheered on my friends and prepared for senior season on the baseball diamond. As life would have it, dedicating an entire year to baseball training still didn't secure a path to collegiate glory. My team was successful and we won a lot, but I just wasn't a huge part of the on-field success. But for some reason, I was convinced my college athlete dreams weren't dead.

Maybe this was a fire God lit in my heart, or maybe I was just not willing to let go of a childhood prayer and dream.

To this day, one of my most vivid high school memories is our baseball team's last game—I sat on the hood of my car for hours afterward, even after the lights had turned off. Our league playoffs were at UofL's field, Cardinal Stadium, and I just sat in the parking lot—completely at a loss. My mom tried to comfort me by reminding me baseball wasn't over, and in just a few weeks I'd be back at that exact same stadium as a manager. I had no way to understand what I was feeling, because it was so much more than my team losing or my competitive playing career being over.

I was lost—for the first time in my life I had to face the reality that my identity was gone as an athlete or baseball player. This left me empty and confused. I was convinced that as a freshman in college, my identity would be all about my past and nothing about my present. The friends I made growing up were because of sports. Nearly all of the memories I had, in some way, were surrounded by sports and being an athlete. Now what?

Seriously, now what? I went to school and assumed my role on the UofL baseball team as an equipment manager. And it wasn't until October of my freshman year that all 6'3, 175lbs of me started to get an unfamiliar nudge.

Perhaps, in that month, the seedling prayer I prayed for so long finally started to take root. By that point, I knew I was nowhere near talented enough to play for a baseball team that would eventually go on to play in the College World Series that season. But the feeling I received that October was a different feeling— a desire to play for a different team.

I'll divulge more details about my decision to transition from baseball to football, while at the University of Louisville, a little later in the book. But for now, here's the short version.

I first tried out for the Louisville football team in January of my freshman year. It was an unsuccessful attempt. After a private workout or two with the long-snapper at the time, I tried out again that spring and ended up making the team.

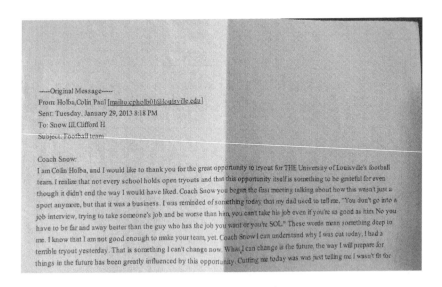

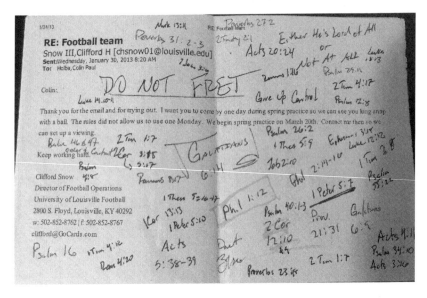

From there, a late growth spurt helped this long-snapping hopeful stand out at a football-worthy 6'5, 245lbs: a frame that was enough to help me make the team and earn a scholarship. After a blessed, healthy, and consistent career, I caught the eye of NFL Scouts—so much that I was invited to the Reese's Senior Bowl, which led to the NFL Combine, and eventually the NFL Draft where I was selected in the 6th round by the Pittsburgh Steelers.

That small little prayer of becoming a college athlete had turned into some Cinderella fantasy of becoming the first draft pick from UofL in the 2017 NFL Draft. It was amazing—beyond any real life experience I could have ever imagined.

Now for a different kind of real life experience.

After training camp in 2017 with the Steelers, I was, to my surprise, released from the team. How quickly things change in the NFL—I went from Mike Tomlin calling me to deliver the most surreal news in April, to being released, jobless and confused in September. On top of a mountain in the spring and in a deep valley come fall—all with a couple of short phone calls.

In my time between tryouts and signing with another team, I needed a part-time job. Enter something I had prepared for my entire life (please hear the sarcasm): I went back into a classroom as a substitute teacher.

Step back into your own world as a 14-year-old. Substitute teachers, especially if it was just for one day, served as a possibility for classmates to bend the rules. With that knowledge, I tried my best to maintain calm in the classroom as a substitute, but sometimes had to meet them in the middle.

On various occasions I used music as a useful compromise. The age of the class determined how much control I'd give them over the music playlist. Kids constantly asked what I liked to listen to, and I would reply with, "Everything, literally everything."

Yes, even Taylor Swift and Katy Perry have made it onto my Apple music playlists—what can I say . . . they create jam after jam.

LEAP!

One song in particular made it onto many student playlists. (And, admittedly, a few personal playlists from time to time). Though I didn't write this book based on a few Katy Perry lines, the following words carry weight—about someone who is feeling stuck or even mildly depressed.

Do you ever feel like a plastic bag
Drifting through the wind, wanting to start again?
Do you ever feel, feel so paper thin
Like a house of cards, one blow from caving in?
Do you ever feel already buried deep?
Six feet under screams, but no one seems to hear a thing.

—Katy Perry, "Firework"

Please stop what you are doing. If you only read those words, go back and sing it this time. I sang it to myself while I was writing. That's right, while starting my book—this dream of mine—I sang them out loud. If you know the melody and chorus (don't lie to yourself, you know it), it's super upbeat and happy. And then if you watch the music video and truly listen to the lyrics, it gets really sad and frustrating to think about being out of control and unhappy with your life.

Obviously, the song is an anthem proclaiming ourselves as "fireworks."

Perry's words mean we're given a unique glow all to ourselves and without our contribution(s) to society, everyone's lives around us wouldn't be as bright.

The song ends as an encouragement to show how special everyone is and how valuable *you* are. That's fantastic, and if you

21

are feeling more than just stuck and struggling with mental battles, I encourage you to not feel any type of way, but to seek conversation, find community and possibly turn to professional help.

Not to be a Debbie Downer, but we've all had moments where it feels like we're just floating around in life—like a plastic bag. When the spark or passion for whatever we're "called to" isn't there. When the responsibility piled onto our plates makes us feel stuck. In those moments, there is no distinct answer on what you should do or who you should do it with—something people refer to as "paralysis by analysis." We are told to go conquer the world, yet when we're in the middle of life's day-to-day grind, it's hard to tell where the starting line is.

But maybe you *know* what your passion is in life. Maybe you are lucky enough to know what your heart desires and you pursue it with everything you have. For the first year, maybe even five years, it was fulfilling and fruitful in your life. But eventually you feel bored—like you're on autopilot just waiting for the weekend so you can really live. Then Sunday comes around and it's back onto the hamster wheel.

But is there something more? Is there something bigger than what's in front of you today?

When God was creating you in your mother's womb, He already knew you. He knew the platform that you would have, your gifts and talents, and how you would love others with those attributes. Day after day, we rob ourselves of the joy God has placed in us because we spend our time, first, comparing ourselves and circumstances to other people. Then we spend energy trying to control who we are. We find our identities wrapped up in the wrong thing and lose focus of who we are and the purpose God has given us.

All of that happens so fast that we don't even know how we got to a place of feeling stuck—sleepwalking through life. Or feeling scared that we have to be something we're not meant to be.

This is how I felt as an equipment manager for the UofL baseball team.

I was so focused on planning my career as a walk-on for the baseball team, but it just wasn't the right fit. So many things happen in life that take our trust away from God and result in *us* controlling the narrative. That feeling, for me, led to a position of being stuck.

I've attended tryouts with many NFL organizations (oftentimes getting a phone call in the middle of the day and on a plane later that night, not knowing when I'd be back), and on more occasions than not I didn't get signed by a team. With a disappointed tone of voice, I would tell my wife each time and could always hear the mix of emotions on her end, too. I just wanted God to show me what was next. Like an arrow pulled back in a bow—that he would just point me in the right direction and let me fly. The issue with that analogy: I was constantly trying to take the bow from God, while simultaneously assuming the position as an arrow.

So, there's the juxtaposition: Can we live a fulfilling life for God *while* also trying to play the same role as Him?

We cannot live both a life for God and be in control.

It is in this mindset that the feeling of being stuck is created. It is in this mindset that comparison is born, and it is in this mindset that we lose the childlike joy of life and allow the weight of responsibility to weigh us down.

The rest of this book is not only my journey and walk with God, but other stories that remind us He is faithful. The journey is one of a call to action—it is a call out of our comfort zone and one that will take us places we never thought we would go. That's just it though: you will never know what God has waiting for you on the other side if you don't trust Him and Leap!

CHAPTER 2

"When we feel stuck, going nowhere—even starting to slip backward—we may actually be backing up to get a running start." —Dan Millman

From time to time, my home church in Louisville has pastors from other churches come speak. One of the most impactful guests they've had, and whom I gleaned much wisdom from, was Albert Tate.

Tate, Lead Pastor at Made for Fellowship church in Los Angeles, has spoken the following statement on multiple occasions—including the time he visited our church:

"God has not taken you this far just to leave you where you are at."

Such a simple yet empowering statement. I think about all of the wonderful blessings God has given Lauren and myself— each other, our careers (although up-and-down at times), our family, friends and experiences. All of which, if I tried to take full-credit for, would make me look like a crazy person.

God has worked too clearly in our lives to just attribute it all to "luck." Yet through it all, I found myself, multiple times throughout my early 20's, looking in the mirror and wondering if I had peaked. Seriously, it got so bad that I even asked guys in my bible study if they had thought that about themselves—just to gauge the room.

That kind of questioning is a slippery slope of the mind. I would look at all God had done and compare it with the things I could take credit for. My heart and mind were so warped that I went back to the drawing board. What, in my mind, led me to where I experienced success?

Hard work, determination, and focus.

Those things were easy to revisit because those were things I had control over—they weren't traits like trust, faith, or patience that all come from God alone. Even my prayer life took a back seat when thinking about the success I could recreate for myself.

The only time I quit football, after my high school junior year season, I never looked back on that decision. Not in the summers during normal conditioning or in the stands my senior year. When I arrived on the UofL campus in August of 2012, the thought of anything football-related wasn't even a twinkle in my eye.

God doesn't always give us full context for why things are happening the way they are in the moment. It's usually not until months or years down the line we see where and why He was working in certain ways. Looking back now, I see He had laid the groundwork for my Leap back at freshman orientation. Back when everyone asked me if I played baseball because I purposefully wore UofL baseball shirts the whole weekend.

"No," I said, "I'm a manager. Just for this season, though. I'm going to work out with them and know what it takes to make the team for next year."

That was the response I had—not because I was spinning some story, but because it is what I truly believed. God had other plans, introducing me to a freshman quarterback, Kyle Todd, and starting a friendship that would play a bigger role in our lives than we knew at the time. As I plotted my way onto the baseball team, God was behind the scenes all along, introducing me to people like Kyle and Aaron Nance—both who would play massively important roles in the events that changed my life.

During my freshman year, my mentality on hard work began to shift. Instead of hard work being a tool I needed for God's plan to unfold, hard work was the crutch I leaned on. In other words, I thought "God's got me this far, but I can take it from here. After all, I worked hard for this."

Once I felt the nudge to try and walk on to the football team, I understood what it was going to take. Even though I didn't have the talent to make the baseball team, I was able to see the work it took to be a successful NCAA Division One athlete. Watching the guys, there was a common theme: hard work. Not just high school hard work like putting in a few extra reps before heading home to play video games. *Real* hard work like staying after practice everyday to work on your struggling attributes. And literally having the mentality that you would do everything in your power everyday to get just 1% better everyday.

That is what I saw pay off for those guys, and so that is what I did.

To wake up in the early hours of the morning, eat and work out before my classes and baseball manager responsibilities kicked in. That was my new life. The nights I did laundry, I would long-snap footballs into a wall by myself, trying to relearn the skill I once enacted in high school.

This was the hard work I came to crave.

There was *control* over what I ate in the morning. There was *control* over the good grades I received. And there was *control* over the preparation necessary to one day tryout for the football team. All while fulfilling my role as baseball manager. To me, this was hard work at play and a sense of control despite the resulting outcome.

Eventually, even after failing football tryouts *twice*, I made the team on my third attempt.

From then on, yes, I knew God was at work in the things out of my control, but it became clear to me that hard work and a sense of control might pay off after all.

That thought, in itself, is not a bad one.

Many preachers say God is going to give you the tools but He can't do the work for you. A parable comes to mind: three men are given money, and the first two invested it (worked hard) and were rewarded. The third buried it in the ground, and was punished for doing nothing with his gift. God requires action on our part, but a healthy mindset recognizes our action is simply the engine. The engine in a car cannot steer or even press the pedal. It takes someone in real control of the entire car to fulfill its purpose, otherwise you end up just revving the engine and going nowhere.

Hard work, in my mind, had short and long-term reinforcements. The same mindset I saw as a manager, I put into play as a football walk-on.

This was a success. I went from needing three different tryouts (just to make the team) to lettering in my second year on the team—which led to a full-ride scholarship, and an eventual NFL draft pick. On the surface, I could take credit for all of that. I had prayed God would allow me to be a D1 athlete, but it was my work ethic on the team that led to success.

College and the NFL are not the same, though. My hard work got me in the door, but everyone worked on another level. And if an NFL player doesn't work hard, they either don't last long in the league or fade to the background on any given team.

The characteristic I used to hang my hat on was now just the standard among each of my colleagues. The more I realized hard work wasn't enough, the more I felt stuck, and even allowed doubt to creep into my mind. This anxiety wasn't anything I could see or hear other people talking about. It wasn't about a test score or if someone liked me or not. It was anxiety wrapped up in how I could sustain a life that provided for my wife and our new family unit.

Those questions, fears, and ghosts stemmed from my anxiety of not being able to "top" what I did next. I had sucked myself down into the pit of self-reliance. A pit cloaked in hard work and determination, but spiked with fear, disappointment, and worry. The scariest part was that the more that I would dig and try to get out, the deeper I found myself.

"What do I want to do? I can't see myself doing this or that. How is that job going to look on my resume? That's not the 5 year plan I had in my head."

We trick ourselves into thinking we don't compare ourselves to others. But a trait as toxic as comparison works subtly and over time, and it's how I had come to push myself toward "success" for all of the wrong reasons.

Last year, in the midst of a pandemic and no NFL teams calling me for a tryout, I had a conversation with a friend on the phone —again, an instance of God using human relationships to get oneself back on track. The question my friend posed ended up being the seed that needed to be planted.

"Colin, what are you passionate about?"

My answer to him shows how deep I was in a pit of self-reliance.

"What I'm passionate about doesn't matter—because I'm passionate about people, but how can I monetize that passion?"

Writing that sentence now, as I reflect on that phone call and season of life, it all makes me laugh. What kind of a response was that? I love people, but could never find a way to make a living off that reality?

The people I look up to don't make an impact solely because of a passion for people, rather a passion for The Lord. Their pursuit of God gave them hearts to help and share their talents with others, and God made a way for them to do it.

I didn't realize my ignorant answer at that moment. And I don't beat myself over it now—my friend didn't either. He was there, on that call, to listen and help me process. But I do know I was just too focused on my own control. And from a 10,000 feet view, that's not an evil motive. But when you take a look at where my heart was, it was about *me* having control over *my* life. The plan I had in *my* head.

To unearth my unhealthy self-reliance, and begin leaning into what God had in store for my future—football or no football—I had to go back a few years before that freshman year in college.

I had to put on my swim trunks again, and walk up to the diving board.

CHAPTER 3

"Anxiety does not empty tomorrow of its sorrows, but only empties today of its strength." —Charles Spurgeon

One of the first memories I have of growing up is going to a local swimming pool.

We went all the time, but there are a few specific moments that stick out above the rest.

Cutting my pinky toe at the pool, as a 5-year-old, and not telling anyone about it. The cut turned into an infection and evolved as lymphangitis. There's something about needing to be held down by five nurses to get shot with a 12-inch needle that just sticks with you for life. My mom told me on the way home that "We'll laugh about this later!" which I guess is partly true because I find the story comical enough to include in this book.

Another memory: soft pretzels. We ate soft pretzels every single day when we got home from the pool one summer—the microwavable kind. This wasn't some tradition passed down, or even repeated during following summers. But one summer in particular, we ate soft pretzels every day and that memory has stuck with me.

Those memories may seem insignificant in the grand scheme of life. I am not really even sure why the CPU between my ears has kept them, but it has.

Yet there is *another* memory.

A memory I *do* think has significant meaning for my life. One that I think *you* can glean from as well. You might even have a similar story as it includes a commonly held fear pertaining to one's youth. This memory is more than just one day—it's more than just a soft pretzel I would dip into mustard before passing out from exhaustion. This memory has more than a few times been a metaphor for my life.

Being four years younger than my brother, I was constantly on a mission to keep up. In everything we did, I wanted to be able to hang out with him growing up. That reality was fueled even more when people would tell me, at some point in puberty's timeline, I was going to be bigger than he was. We played every sport under the sun, and for a four-year age gap between us, he was pretty patient with me.

Naturally, I wanted to swim in the deep end with him and his friends during those summer afternoons at the pool. I was seven years old, and the day came where I asked to join him and his buddies. First, I had to pass the swim test which would give me access to spend an afternoon playing "sharks and minnows" in the deep end.

There was one obstacle that stood in my way:

At our pool, there was a diving board.

Now, as an adult, I look at diving boards without much thought. To be honest, I've kinda become that stereotypical adult at the pool—not wanting to get splashed by kids absolutely loving their lives on a hot summer day. (Man, just writing that makes me sound so old and lame).

But at age seven? That diving board was no doubt the biggest obstacle of my little life.

At age six, I had broken my wrist which I never saw as a real problem. The lymphangitis shot with five nurses holding me down? Maybe a problem at the moment but the infection would pass.

The crazy part is that a little diving board *shouldn't* have been an issue. I passed the swim test and my parents told my brother to stay by the landing area to help me up if I needed it. In so many ways, I was covered. There were even a few who, on the day I passed the swim test and approached the diving board, were encouraging me to do it.

"You got this, Colin!"

"Go for it, Colin! Then you can play in the deep end with us!"

This is where my short story turns into a divine comedy. One day turned to two, and two days turned into multiple weeks that summer. Each time we would go to the pool, I would spend the car ride over psyching myself up, telling myself that "Today is the day."

My mom or dad would tell me I could do it. And each time, I would get in line, wait my turn, climb the three stairs, inch out toward the edge of the teal, industrial-grade metal and look out at the deep blue water.

And then I would stand there.

Frozen in time.

My eyes locked with the bottom of the swimming pool floor. Surely, I thought, that floor seemed lower than when I swam in the deep end for my test.

"What if I get water in my nose?"

"What if I sink too far down and can't hold my breath to get back up?"

My mind flooded with paralyzing thoughts of "What if?"

One friend suggested I sit on the edge, curl up in a ball and just roll off. Another suggested as soon as I finished climbing up the stairs to just keep running until my feet ran overboard.

But nothing could stop the thoughts from grabbing my mind and taking control.

Over time, my excitement for the pool in general started to wane. I was haunted by past defeat, worry, and fear. Such vivid memories of standing at the end of the board until the person behind me finally ran out of patience:

"Hey! Get off the board so we can go already!"

Funny how insignificant words stick with you growing up.

My fear became infused with embarrassment. How had this spiraled so far out of control? All I wanted was to join my brother and his friends in their cannonball competitions. I had all of the support and green lights necessary to jump. Our pool was a source of joy and excitement, but to me it had turned into a place of shame, embarrassment, and anxiety. I grew defensive of others asking, "Colin, are you going to do it? Are you going to jump today?"

Of course I wanted to jump. Why would I have put myself through that situation so many times? To get in line, climb the ladder, and stand at the edge. These simple questions over the course of time, in my own head, had gone from curiosity to ridicule.

Throughout childhood, we're introduced to these experiences meant to bring us joy—meant to fill us with laughter and fun memories. Of all the times I have now jumped off a diving board, there are none that stand out. Truth be told, I can't even remember the specific time I did jump off for the first time.

I contemplated creating an anecdote, for dramatic effect as a climax to this chapter, to explain the rush of relief that came with finally jumping off.

But that wouldn't be true to my story. It wouldn't be authentic.

Maybe my parents remember, yet it clearly wasn't a momentous occasion. But here's what I do remember: all of those feelings. The embarrassment, anxiety, and worry of being paralyzed and *stuck* right at the edge of that board. I don't remember that first jump, but what I do know is there has not been a single time since that I have stepped on a diving board and experienced any of those seven-year-old emotions. There are no flashbacks or waves of remembrance of not being able to do it. *That*—from age seven to 77—is what God wants with our mental state.

We can have days, weeks, months, or even years of crippling fear that turns into mental paralysis. We feel stuck in those places because we don't see how we can get ourselves out.

That's the hurdle to get over—the way out isn't simple, but boils down to trusting God enough to take the Leap He has placed in front of you. Sometimes it is just getting to that breaking point and Leaping, because at some point it's about the only thing you have left to do.

God calls us to a life of action. The Gospel isn't just full of parables, but Jesus himself feeding and healing—walking on water and calling his disciples to do the same.

They, too, probably only saw the metaphorical pool floor.

But zoom out to everyone in history, in the bible or otherwise, who was called to pursue something bigger than themselves.

First came fear. And then came a Leap that changed everything.

CHAPTER 4

"The most important thing is to try and inspire people so that they can be great in whatever they want to do." —Kobe Bryant

With a background in sports, I'm aware that "success" is at the foundation of most things anyone might pursue. Many authors, athletes, artists and entrepreneurs possess a similar bent —a similar pursuit of excellence at their craft, creating for a streamlined path toward success.

Think about the rule of 10,000.

The 10,000 reps of hitting a golf shot, 10,000 times practicing the guitar, writing 10,000 words or 10,000 minutes spent speaking in public, or 10,000 long snaps into a laundry-room wall.

To become proficient at something, we've all heard it might take at least 10,000 reps or practice opportunities to achieve mastery-level understanding and performance.

But in the middle of all those reps, you must understand: we don't arrive at any destination *without* passion fueling us amidst the ups and downs.

Motivational speaker and *New York Times Bestseller*, Jon Gordon, talks about how he writes and prepares for books and speaking engagements. He carves out a minimum of an hour a day, for weeks on end, to write in preparation. Sometimes he just writes whatever comes into his mind, sometimes he writes with a purpose to complete a speech or an article, and other times he sits down with seemingly nothing on his mind to talk about. One thing that's evident: he lets the Holy Spirit wash through him to cover pages of material.

But it feels appropriate to talk about how we get to the point of taking these Leaps.

The diving board did not just happen, and probably wouldn't be a memory if it hadn't solicited strong feelings of fear. Walking onto the football team at UofL wouldn't have happened had I gotten everything I prayed for in high school. Time and time again, the idea of "timing" pops up. For me, especially with God, timing is a double edged sword.

The first edge is what we do with our own time.

I bring up the rule of 10,000 because I do believe that there is work on our part. I don't think God is in heaven counting out our reps saying, "Ok . . . 9,998, 9,999, annnd 10,000. Now Colin is ready."

However, He is waiting on our hearts to become ready. There are experiences we must go through to prepare us for what lies ahead. Humbling moments, life experiences, perceptions of humanity and the path God has in store for us. I would never have stuck with football if I hadn't experienced being a collegiate baseball manager. I would never have truly experienced God speaking to me if I had never gone on Bible and Beach (a trip I took through my church my senior year of high school). When I tried out and didn't make the football team the first time, I needed God to speak and tell me, "This is part of the plan, Colin."

Do not worry about how it is going to happen, but just keep doing your part. I don't think that there are 10,000 reps for figuring out your calling, but there is an experiential aspect to it. God needs our hearts primed for anything—good or bad. The course of action we take in life can lead to a longer or shorter path, but we don't just arrive without preparation.

Such is the *earthly* side of this double edged sword.

This is the action happening in front of us. We watch what may appear as random events—good, bad or indifferent. We watch many of those moments pass by with insignificant lenses until hindsight reveals their purposes. The second edge is a more blunt edge—one that is never swift or easy to process, and is measured with tough, patient love.

Heavenly timing never seems to line up with our own.

Getting released, fired, or rejected for the umpteenth time never comes with a side of "This is all for God's plan."

The unexpected rejection, or the feeling of waiting for rain in the desert, doesn't get easy. The 10,000th time you pray and ask for God to reveal His plan might bring deafening radio silence . . . that blow from the sword never gets easier. Friends and family try to comfort us throughout our trials, pointing out that God has a plan, and that whatever your life is leading to is part of His plan.

That doesn't get easier to hear.

If the first part of the sword is the free will we possess to move forward and complete the work God has given us, the second edge of the sword is the opportunity we are given to *trust* God with our Leap. Speaking for myself, the more my responsibilities grew, the more I wanted to turn away from this "tough love from above." Trying out for the football team was easy—if I didn't make it, I was still a student and manager on the baseball team. I was fairly certain I had those things to fall back on. My NFL career, on the other hand, has come with a loving wife, a child on the way, a home, monthly bills and all the other responsibilities of "adulting."

"God, you seem to be taking some time off fulfilling my wants and needs, so I'll take over for now and we can touch base later."

That spiral of thought is not unnatural as we age. It's not wrong to pursue goals as a worthy husband, father, and provider. But you have to check your mindset daily.

Is a spouse pursuing work success a worthy spouse? Or is the spouse who is pursuing God something we should desire even more-so? What is the desired balance of the two?

These appear as easy, rhetorical questions. Yet we constantly fum-

ble with the answers. I wait patiently for approval from earthly standards—what others expect of me—and become impatient when waiting for God's timing.

God is not causing harm to us, rather He is spending this time to shape us, mold us, and allow us free will. Yet, He is also constantly refining us into the men and women He has called us to be. Selfishly, we sometimes think of waiting as God forgetting about us. But how quickly we forget! God loves us so much He sent His son to die for us.

Jesus himself cried out "Abba Father, if there is any other way, please let this cup pass from me."

Jesus, too, heard silence in the midst of God's plan.

But our prayers do not go unheard—we just can't see the forest through the trees.

Much of 2020 I spent riding a stationary bike—yes, oftentimes with a mask. People at my gym knew I was trying to get back under contract and had heard about some of my tryouts. They'd kindly ask how I was doing and feeling about the process amid COVID uncertainties. For some reason, I'd point to the stationary bike and explain "This is the metaphor for my life. I can work hard or ride easy. I can be inspired for a moment and work myself out of breath, but no matter how hard I do or don't try, when I get off this bike I have gone absolutely nowhere."

This was my view on life. I wanted to continue to play in the NFL but couldn't get signed. I wanted to know my direction and felt lost in the process.

Shooting from the hip, I applied for a Special Agent position with the FBI—went through a few rounds of the long interview process only to get rejected, again. I had been racking my brain for what the heck I was going to do whenever I was done with football or more realistically, when football decided it was done with me. I never came up with a concrete answer.

So I started a masters degree, only to get the funding for my degree pulled right after my first day of classes. There was no good answer for anything, and my life seemed to hit a stand still. No matter how hard I tried, how hard I worked, or how bad I wanted anything—at the end of each day there was nothing to show for my efforts.

I pedaled so hard. But I was stationary.

Towards the end of summer 2020, the pastor at my home church, Kyle Idleman, was doing a sermon series on the gospel of John.

The imagery of me on my stationary bike was embossed into my brain—clearly it was, as it's the first thing I shared with gym-goers who inquired about my situation. Kyle talked about the Holy Spirit. He talked about how we should pray God might lead us, fill us, and show us the path of life.

"You make known to me the path of life; you will fill me with joy in your presence, with eternal pleasures at your right hand." —Psalm 16:11, NIV

COLIN HOLBA

Yet as Christians, Kyle proclaimed, we are filled with the Holy Spirit. Jesus even said to his disciples that he was leaving this world but someone better was going to come after.

"And I will ask the Father, and he will give you another advocate to help you and be with you forever— the Spirit of truth. The world cannot accept him, because it neither sees him nor knows him. But you know him, for he lives with you and will be in you." —John 14:16-17, NIV

It hit me that we cry out for Jesus to heal us and guide us but don't address the fact God is literally with us at all times through the Holy Spirit. That reality struck a chord in me. I had felt so distanced from God, and sitting in a Sunday service pew was reminded God is living inside of me—no Follower of Christ can ignore this.

Those words alone from Kyle could have sent me on a mission out of the church doors—inspired and ready to take on the week ahead with renewed vigor and confidence in the Spirit. But it was the story he told after reading through excerpts of John that created a small crack in my wall of control—that eventually led to the flood of inspiration for picking up a pen (or typing on a keyboard) and writing this book.

Kyle talked about flying a kite.

In our childhoods, flying a kite might not be as common as going to the pool, but every listener can resonate with his visualization and ensuing analogy.

On a windy day, there isn't much you have to do to fly a kite. Run a little bit, yes, and let it catch the wind before hanging onto the adventure to come. Something so simple. Conversely, on a day you wanted to fly your kite *without* any wind, you could spend hours and a countless amount of energy running and throwing your kite into the air to try—compelling it to take off and catch wind ... even if just for a moment.

But with no wind, all your efforts would never amount to the experience of flying on a windy day. When nature does the work for you—the wind blows over the grass and takes control of the kite from your hands, handle, and string. You think you spent a lot of energy to get this whole thing in motion, but it's the wind that took a lifeless kite and threw it up into the sky. For a kite to soar overhead is something, in all of our efforts, no one could ever accomplish alone.

This is the Holy Spirit working in us.

To me, this imagery changed absolutely everything. It's what I needed to get off my (literal and figurative) stationary bike of self-pity and run outside. The stationary bike wasn't taking me anywhere, nor could it—It was all about *my* movement and *my* statistical progress, with no interaction among others and no real place to go.

But a kite . . . even if it didn't take off right away, there was always a hope that at a moment there would be a breath from the heavens to lift my sails, and all I had to do was hold on.

When I started thinking about this in a practical way, I thought about the notion of taking a leap of faith. Leaping involves effort from us, but at some point (rather quickly, for me, at 245lbs) gravity will pull you back down. I want to change the idea around a "leap of faith."

A true Leap is just what takes the control away from you.

When we are off the ground, we have no control—we are in a sense floating and that's where God needs us. He doesn't want to drag us to His calling for us, that is why He gives us free will. However, when we humbly release control, and allow ourselves to Leap, flight is a real possibility. And just as the birds in the air can cover oceans and not grow weary, or be defined by earthly rules of gravity, we will feel the wind lift us off our feet.

In that moment, God will take us to places we never dreamed of going and will provide us experiences outside our walls of belief.

Your pending Leap will give your kite life! The Spirit is ready and willing. Are you?

PART 2

CHAPTER 5

*"You are never too old to set another goal or
to dream a new dream."* —C.S. Lewis

Something that doesn't translate very well to most people is that, professional sports aren't exactly what you think they are —I've come to find nearly all professional athletes and entertainers feel this in some way.

Oftentimes, there are sacrifices to be made not only by you, but by many of your family and friends. Graduations, funerals, weddings and holidays will routinely take a back seat to gameday demands. So many times I have tried to tell myself that football wasn't my identity, but with all that it requires from everyone around you, it is so hard to truly keep your identity. A constant battle between what I do and who I am.

After I was drafted and the initial excitement wore off, Lauren and I (we were dating at the time) had to start thinking about how this would impact her career: would she follow me? Would we break up? Where would she apply to medical school? Would she still apply to med school? This was just the first wave of hard conversations and selflessness Lauren endured for me and my dream—all for me to not even make the Steelers roster out of training camp.

I started a collection of odd jobs when not on an NFL team. For two seasons, I juggled the life of a substitute teacher and substitute NFL long snapper—filling in for teachers on maternity leave and other long snappers who were hurt or suspended. Though I felt welcomed in each respective school and NFL organization, I never felt like they were places I could plant roots, find stability, or see Lauren and I building a home.

Especially as a substitute teacher.

God bless teachers. As someone who has a background in finance and never pictured himself on that side of the desk, high schoolers have a quick way of challenging and humbling you.

The start of my third NFL season in 2019 is when I thought I had a chance to settle in and really become a part of a team —I made the San Francisco 49ers squad out of training camp, and finally felt it was going to be my place. It may have taken a couple extra years, but finally we had "arrived." Lauren was finishing school and on pace for a great job the following summer, and I was going to be a 49er.

It's funny how those dreams seem nice for a little before they don't play out nearly the way you thought they would.

I played the first two games as a San Francisco 49er with the second being in Cincinnati against the Bengals—close to my home in Louisville—where I had the biggest collection yet of friends and family at a game. All to get on a plane back to California, get released, and hop on a red eye flight back home to Louisville.

Unemployed and yet again waiting and praying, "God, what is going on? What is the point in all of this?"

I was blessed to sign and play with the New York Giants just a few weeks later. Again, we started thinking about New York as a place where we could really see our family living for a while. Seemingly, it checked all of the boxes for us: direct flight home, plenty of work opportunities for Lauren, and another shot at playing the game I love. It just didn't check the box of God's plan for more than a few games. It was a blessing, without a doubt, it just wasn't in God's long-term plan for us.

After the season ended, I was released from the Giants a few weeks into a global pandemic without any prospective work-outs or opportunities to prove myself. As I reflect on that time, I know I sank into a depressed state.

I was tired of feeling like I was letting my wife down—like she couldn't depend on me and this career she had already sac-rificed so much for. I was done with hearing "No" or "Good job, we just don't have a need for you." I was sick of getting calls from an "Unknown Number" telling me if I'm getting on a flight and where to, and for how long, and do I have a chance to make this or that team. I was exhausted after coming home from workouts and with nothing to show for it, other than added stress for Lauren and myself.

I turned to spending money to make myself feel good.

"Oh, I can have another drink because it's my birthday."

"Oh, I can play a round of golf at this expensive course."

Even when we moved into our new home, I had hope, but knew the place itself wouldn't bring me joy. That came from within, which I could find none.

There was an endless pattern: my family consistently showed love and support, but I felt like it was never enough because of my own mindset and insecurities. I was lost—the year 2020 felt like, for me, the same spot as a high school senior, sitting on the hood of my car for hours . . . empty and lost.

Now, not only had I hitched my wagon to football success, but my wife had made life-altering decisions following me in the process—deciding where to live or apply to schools, and ultimately turning down medical school to become a nurse. All of this weighed heavily, and, if I'm honest, *still* gets to me if I think too long and hard about it. But through it all, those thoughts and feelings are built on a foundation of *gratitude* and I truly hope you have others in your life who you can say the same about.

I take the time to share all this as a background of who I really am.

Rest assured, the whole of this book is not some soap box or manifesto. Part of what's written is a way to navigate through thoughts and emotions. To list out all of the ways that God has proved Himself to be trustworthy to my wife and I time and time again, and yet still time and time again we look for reassurance that God is there and hasn't forgotten about us. I am a broken and messy man. I have sinned and lost my way so many times. I have tried to take control when I felt God didn't have it. My wife and I have experienced conflict in regard to what is next and if we trusted each other in the process. Plenty of more things disqualify me from being an "expert" husband, friend, or Christian . . .

That's the beauty of this life that we are all blessed with. Nobody is set apart as better or worse than the next. We are all searching for more trust and control. We constantly need reassurance, forgiveness and grace. When you hear that little voice or feel that nudge to move in the right direction, you don't have to fix who you are—you are being called to take a Leap right where you are. Even if right where you are feels like a state of drowning.

Have you ever felt that way? As if you were being swallowed by waves and completely out of control in the process?

For whatever reason, work is getting to be too much and it just keeps piling up. The waves of life come crashing in. The waning moon makes those waves bigger. The safety of sand sometimes leaves us beaten down, soaked and wandering in the darkness —we wonder when the light will come and cause a break. And then there's the wind.

For much of my adult life, the Holy Spirit has revealed Itself to me as wind.

You can feel the wind and sense its impact on the world around you, but you can't control it, stop it, hold it, or see it. You simply are a being amongst the wind.

Grace, on the other hand, has revealed itself to me as water. Both water and wind can represent something of great peace and calming. Together, the perfect amount can create story-book imagery in our minds. The sound of a slow, babbling brook as water lilies dance—while a spring breeze whispers. Amidst the heat of day, the calm waters refresh you and the breath of earth dries you off. When all five of our senses are touched by water and wind, they work together to create a feeling of paradise. There are moments—hopefully many moments —when this is God for us. The oasis you need in life to get away, to recharge and to refocus on advancing His kingdom.

Wind and water together don't always paint this picture for people.

Hurricane Katrina, or subsequent hurricanes Irma, Dorian, and Maria. These names for many people convey nothing but destruction and heartache. All are a result of disproportionate amounts of wind and water mixed with earthly destruction. Yet time and time again, such stormy imagery represents the people of God and the stories of our lives. In the midst of the storm, where is God?

Where is His grace after my house is ripped away from me? Where is His mercy while I hold the hand of my dying child? How can I trust God when my prayers are being washed away by tears, and for years I can't see change?

To many people, these are their memories—metaphorically or literally—when they think not only of God but of the Holy Spirit. So many times we lean on our own understanding. Instead of leaning in, we border up. We nail windows shut, we evacuate for a time . . . only to come back to what we left. Once we board up our doors and nail the plywood to windows, we wonder if we should ever take them off again. We know the storm will come again, and those precautions protect us. In the midst of a storm—force that we *cannot* control—we lean into our sense of control. We do everything to secure a feeling of protection.

"I can board up my house and protect it. I can evacuate and clean up the mess when I come back. I can fix what has been destroyed by

this storm."

The sense of control over the storm gives us comfort in areas that we cannot contain.

Throughout the rest of Part Two, I want to examine the lives of three individuals who walked on this earth and encountered such storms. There are more examples I'll use to supplement their stories, but it's so important to note how every person in the Bible that God used started off as an ordinary person. Even Jesus was born in an old, undesirable manger.

There are many lessons to unpack, but the notion of Leaping has been around for thousands of years, so why not look at the way they responded to God when the storm came calling?

Although water and wind wreak havoc in a hurricane, we know, as noted earlier in this chapter, they can also bring peace and calm. As you read the pages ahead, keep a few questions in the back of your mind.

When was the last time I was ever caught in one of life's storms? Am I in a storm right now? Do I sense a storm coming? What are my tendencies in a storm? Do I run to God or something else? Do I run to people or work or something else to fill the fear and void caused by the storm? How did men and women in the Bible, not just the ones listed in this book, react to storms in *their* life? What about the men and women I look up to and respect in my life? How have they reacted in the middle of a storm?

A few questions to get you started—but there might be more.

The point is, before reading these next three chapters, to take a step back and examine how we react to the storms of life—when the wind and rain run rampant and we can't see in front of our face. Those moments, for most humans on earth, seem to be the scariest place in the world.

But if the God of the Bible has shown us anything, it's that those moments might be the reason we were born. The reason we were born to Leap.

CHAPTER 6

"There is peace even in the storm." —*Vincent van Gogh*

The last place God wants us is in a place of self-preservation and safety—to seek out methods and strategies to get out of the storm. Ironically, the more we try to avoid the storm is usually when we end up creating it for ourselves.

Much like the waves for Jonah, the storm serves a purpose. Jonah ran away from God, deliberately opposing what God was calling him to do. The mission was out of Jonah's comfort zone and out of his control. Until God made him lose all sense of control on the boat and in the belly of a fish. The platform Jonah was called to was not something he wanted. The goal, to Jonah, was pointless—those people didn't want to hear about God and they didn't want to know God. Why waste time and put his own life in jeopardy? That wasn't Jonah's plan. And yet, it was the plan that God had for him. Jonah had to get uncomfortable and he had to get wet. But the grace of God first had to run through him.

There is a fascinating sermon illustration about God's grace for us. We hear it so often that God's grace is like a cup running over. I once witnessed a well-known pastor from Lexington take a cup, and while talking would pour it out. He demonstrated how God's cup is poured out into us. Honestly, I zoned out a little bit because my mind filled with a metaphor I had never thought of before. He was pouring the water out of the cup onto a towel on the ground. This made me think that we are the towel. I know that is not what you wanted to hear. If it makes you feel any better, you are a really nice towel—from Costco or maybe one you slipped into your bag from a nice hotel (not that anyone has ever done that). But let's just say you're a cozy, ultra-absorbent towel.

When I feel like I am drowning in the middle of a storm, I tend to focus on myself. I ask myself, "Where can I grab hold of comfortability in this strenuous process?" Generally in a less calm manner than that.

I search for ways people might pour into me, help me and show me grace along the path back to land. That God, in those moments, would open my eyes and show me relief. Instead of taking action, we are often reactionary. In other words, we need help yet refuse to take necessary action. At some point, no matter how nice the towel is, when it becomes oversaturated it loses its purpose. Nobody wants to use a wet towel as they come out of the shower. It isn't warm or dry and it isn't going to help them dry off. Soaked towels don't absorb new water. Rather, that towel needs to be wrung out. It needs to take all of the water that was taken in. That process of wringing out water is uncomfortable—it takes work, but it is the only way for the towel to become effective again.

If we are the towel, and grace is the living water, no wonder we can feel heavy and weighed down. We have become so saturated with grace from God and from brothers and sisters around us that we have made our purpose about ourselves.

We have become comfortable receiving grace, and pouring it out of ourselves has become work.

That act alone—giving others grace—places us outside of our comfort zone. In my conversations with others, I fear that we see comfort and control going hand in hand. Yet nowhere in the Bible or in Jesus' ministry on earth did he seek out comfort *or* control. He was born in a manger—not like a king. He sweated blood as He prayed that the cup of His death may pass from Him. Yet He endured a humiliating and excruciating death on our behalf. The call to His disciples was not for earthly comfort —it was not for them to take control of the church after His ascension, it was for them to spread the message of Jesus to the ends of the earth, making more disciples. This was their purpose. And it is what remains our purpose today too.

The American dream is not what God has called us to. But it's likely what Jonah would have run to had it existed then.

I have fallen into the trap myself. Society paints a picture of the way we are supposed to live. A happy family, a good job and a good house—most likely a dog in the backyard, a nice spot to vacation every year, and take the kids to Disney World at least once in their life. Retire at 65, play a ton of golf, pickleball, or what have you. Focus on your own 401k, creating a better life for your kids than you had—not necessarily because you had a bad life, but because that's what society says you have to do.

The hardest part is you have to plan all of that out. At eighteen years-of-age, you graduate high school and decide where to go to college, what to do in college, or what job to get if you don't go to college. Then you're supposed to meet your spouse in college, and if you don't . . . you better find somebody soon, because you need to hit that target of having kids before age 30 or 35 or whatever the community around you deems is the appropriate age to have kids. Then decide where to live, because you have to manage what schools your kids (that you don't have yet) will attend. What job you'll do for about five years before you leverage that job for a new job. But the new job may take you out of state, or it may call for your spouse or significant other to make a sacrifice for *their* individual life-plan, or worse, they could have a job or school opportunity that makes *you* make a sacrifice. Now that wasn't part of your plan.

If those sentences strike a chord, it's because those sentences should be frustrating to read. They outline pressures(s) many of us face—if not those same situations, the situations themselves are not far off from what I've described.

Where does wind and water fall into the American dream?

Do those elements form an oasis on Sunday when you feel good after going to church? The local church—where you tell yourself you're going to start making a difference, and then you leave and go grocery shopping and watch football and slip right back into your hamster wheel? Or is it the hurricane that has derailed all of those plans, because you're 30 and haven't met the person you're supposed to marry. Or the job you thought you were meant to have never actually became your job, so in your mind you've just been wasting your time at some "stop gap" job until the right one comes along. Those career decisions might stoke the flames of your passion, but what *is* the passion itself? I ask you again: Where does the wind have a chance to breathe when the worry, stress, and control of life has taken its breath out of you?

Our idea of what we are supposed to do has been ingrained in our heads for a multitude of reasons. In all of that anxiety-infused rambling, where is there room for prayer?

"God, prepare my heart, so that I can be a part of advancing your kingdom today. Lord, open my eyes to see your plans. Touch my hands so that I may do your work, and sing through my voice that I can speak your words. Lord reveal to me today how I can advance your kingdom. Please allow my prayer to impact the people around me in a way so that they can know you better, that they can feel love, and grace. Amen."

I am confident that this prayer and the American dream (at least the one of the 21st century) don't go together quite like we're told they do. When you are grounded into the earth, you cannot feel the wind. If you do, you root more—not wanting to blow over or lose control. Yet, this is exactly what the Lord is urging from you.

Take the Leap and let God blow away the fears and stress you have created for yourself.

Become content in the thought and reality of uncomfortability. Jesus has never called you to the five-year plan or a solid 401k. He calls us to trust in Him—to take up our cross and follow him daily. This is not a mental sentiment, rather the most accurate representation we have seen of taking a Leap. Letting the wind sweep us off our feet and carry us to whatever platform God has called us to—no matter how big or small.

I've thought about you, the reader, multiple times throughout this book-writing process. Those last words—on whatever platform God has called you to—is what I've prayed for specifically. Many times in life, I have felt those exact emotions. I may or may not have experienced situations like yours exactly, but we all have felt anguish—as if our prayers aren't answered. I have cried out to God only to finish and feel unheard. Whether that is on a heavenly level or an earthly level, I have been there —and most likely you have, too. One of the worst feelings in the world is feeling rejected. Whether it's work, a relationship, or opportunity . . . being told there is someone better than you never feels good. In my experience, you can't even build a numbness to that feeling or assume indifference. Before I made the football team at UofL, I was told that I wasn't good enough to play for them. In the NFL, I have been cut or had someone else signed over me numerous times. Before my wife, I went on a handful of first dates but very few that ever led to a second.

The feeling of not being enough is something that in one way or another we have all felt, and none of us enjoy or get used to it. There is a feeling of insignificance and a notion that other people have something you don't. At times, there is nothing you can do about it. A sense that being 100% true to yourself just wasn't enough.

A while back, I read *Capital Gaines*—a memoir by *Fixer Upper* television star, Chip Gaines. The book is about his life, triumphs, mistakes, and lessons learned. There is a lot of wisdom in his words, and God certainly has given Chip and his wife, Joanna, a cool platform to impact lives. After reading, I would talk with people about the book and their response was always the same: "Yeah, but that's Chip and Joanna *Gaines*."

I didn't think about their response much, but eventually I sat down to write this book and it hit me.

"That's exactly the point!" I thought to myself as I started punching out words on the keyboard.

They *are* Chip and Joanna Gaines yet if we stepped in a time-machine that took us back to Waco, Texas in 2012, and you lived outside of that city, and I asked you who the Gaines were . . . you would have no idea.

That's what dawned on me. We hear stories about Chip Gaines and countless other people with giant platforms who started off slow, and ultimately took off. They ran into storms early on in life and then one thing changed and those individuals started changing the world—one day at a time.

As I write this chapter, it's Christmas time. I find it funny how the main thing in so many stories, especially the ones that center around a bildungsroman (story about childhood or spiritual formation), highlight a similar theme: one thing changes and that new thing changes the whole story.

Isn't that the same with Jesus and the arc of Christmas, and the Good News of redemption in Christ?

One day, Jesus hadn't ever walked on the earth. The next, he was born into this world on a specific path—as a savior. At the end of his ministry, Jesus was crucified for us and rose three days later so that we might have salvation and hope in eternal life. Before Jesus was born, Jonah had his own bildungsroman life change when his boat was caught in the middle of the storm. Don't think his story was all about a fish—it was about a moment when God got a hold of his attention through any means necessary so that a normal human being could fulfill his purpose on earth, to connect people to God.

This idea—that those people I listed were normal people like you and me—carries weight because they were average individuals. (Well, Jesus was a little different). But, don't get it twisted —just because we are "normal" human beings doesn't mean that you aren't special and created for a purpose. That couldn't be farther from the truth.

How dare we doubt how much God loves us?

We possess worth solely because we are *His*. He made us in His own image and knows us deeply. Why would we think He doesn't have a purpose and a plan for our lives? Like he would leave us in a drowning state?

Your platform can't be the same as other people, how would we reach everyone if that were the case? We all need to embrace our own platform, but just like the body we all serve a massive purpose. Romans 12 even lists out that we are all called to be great in our own areas.

"We have different gifts, according to the grace given to each of us. If your gift is prophesying, then prophesy in accordance with your faith; if it is serving, then serve; if it is teaching, then teach; if it is to encourage, then give encouragement; if it is giving, then give generously; if it is to lead, do it diligently; if it is to show mercy, do it cheerfully." —Romans 12:6-8

A thumb doesn't seem as important as eyes, yet we can hold on to things we see because we have both of those specific body parts. Every platform is important to God, because God intentionally created everything. He created the universe and didn't finish each aspect only to shrug his shoulders and say, "Sure, that'll work." Instead, He diligently created every iota, and at the end of the day, called it good.

For you and I, He did the same thing.

When God created you, He declared you are *good*. You are created with a purpose by God. Your platform will be different because it was designed to be. Jesus died for you so you could fulfill the purpose and platform He created you for. That is how special you are. That is why He wants you to trust him: because he purposefully created you to live for Him and something

COLIN HOLBA

grander than ourselves alone.

CHAPTER 7

"You don't drown by falling into water. You only drown if you stay there." —Zig Ziglar

But Jesus immediately said to them: "Take courage! It is I. Don't be afraid." "Lord, if it's you," Peter replied, "tell me to come to you on the water." "Come," he said. Then Peter got down out of the boat, walked on the water and came toward Jesus. But when he saw the wind, he was afraid and, beginning to sink, cried out, "Lord, save me!" Immediately Jesus reached out his hand and caught him. "You of little faith," he said, "why did you doubt?" And when they climbed into the boat, the wind died down. Then those who were in the boat worshiped him, saying, "Truly you are the Son of God."

—Matthew 14: 27-33

I have spoken with many of my close friends and mentors about how this book is part of my Leap—the book in itself is part of my next chapter. Ultimately, this book is a story of faith. Of coming to a point where you can hear God or tangibly feel Him moving throughout points in your life when you need courage or faith to take that Leap! One of my close friends heard about the idea for this book, and with all sincerity told me the following:

"Colin, make sure to talk about when you take a Leap and it doesn't work out. Make sure this isn't some feel good, self-help book. That's not real or authentic."

His words left a mark.

I am so fired up about this book and helping others secure the courage to move forward, that this friend's advice brought me back to reality.

Consider verses in the bible like John 16:33:

"I have said these things to you," Jesus said, "that in me you may have peace. In the world you will have tribulation. But take heart; I have overcome the world."

Yet those words didn't really summarize a Leap and/or what happens when that Leap falls short in the world's eyes.

For me, I think more often on the life of Peter

Peter is, for me, the most relatable person from the Bible. It comforts me to hear that David is a man after God's own heart, yet struggled mightily and sinned before God and man—even in our present day, we can recognize just how many times he messed up and failed others. Adam, made uniquely by God, had a tangible relationship with God, yet also sinned and struggled. But there is something different that captivates me about Peter. In their own way, each of the aforementioned individuals had a close walk with God—whether in Eden with Him, a journey as

LEAP!

a King, or literally walking and talking with the Messiah. These men were closer to God in ways most humans cannot fathom. It makes them great individuals to study and learn from.

Sometimes I think we get caught up in movies and artistic expression—we lose sight that these men were just that: men, human. From a different time and era, yes, but they were human just like you and me. They had struggles on earth, and were close to God in ways unlike other people, just like you and me. Yes, just like you and me. When Jesus ascended into Heaven, the third part of the Trinity came down to earth: The Holy Spirit. And when we accept Jesus as Lord and Savior, we are literally asking Christ to be with us at all times. Even more so than Adam, Moses, David, and Peter, we are able to be with God 24/7 every moment. They walked and talked with God, and they still struggled—just like us. They weren't *characters* . . . they were humans. They were close to God and not everything worked out for them. They had missteps and fell short. They had moments when, although close to God, felt distant from God. As great and purposeful as their lives were, they at times felt stuck and like God had forgotten about them.

Back to Peter and the passage I noted at the beginning of this chapter—from the book of Matthew. I left out a couple verses from the beginning because I wanted you to read them here instead.

"Immediately Jesus made the disciples get into the boat and go on ahead of him to the other side, while he dismissed the crowd. After he had dismissed them, he went up on a mountainside by himself to pray. Later that night, he was there alone, and the boat was already

69

a considerable distance from land, buffeted by the waves because the wind was against it."

In this story, there may not be a definitive Leap. But there are moments when you don't feel the presence of Jesus and still need to make a move. Think about what Jesus himself does—he goes by himself to pray. This can't be overlooked, when you are in a feeling of being by yourself, out to sea with no sight of land, I urge you to go pray—just like Jesus did. Continue to prepare yourself for when you feel his presence and can hear your purpose being spoken to you. Peter was scared, and then he wanted to jump out of the boat and walk on water with Jesus in excitement. He then got scared and started to rely on himself and his own control, and started to sink. He took the Leap when Jesus presented an opportunity, but he still sank.

Notice how when he started to sink, Jesus helped him up—the story was no longer about Peter walking on the water, they just returned to the boat after Jesus helped him. It wasn't about Peter walking on the water, it wasn't even about Peter's faith to take the Leap. This passage is about Peter's wanting to be with Jesus. About worshipping him.

That might not be what my friend had in mind when he said to mention Leaps that don't work out. But to me, everything has to come back to Jesus, our purpose after all, is connecting people to Jesus and loving them as he showed us.

The Leap isn't easy though, and it isn't a promise that you'll catch the wind. Hearing the call and feeling the urge to Leap is a fantastic sign and next step, but there is continued work: stay the course. Grow closer in faith and trust. The Leap is just the starting point and just because you take it, doesn't mean that you won't sink. But it *does* mean you can be closer to God than before.

As much as we can focus on Peter becoming anxious and losing sight of Jesus when he was walking on water, we need to highlight the physical things that happened. When Peter got out of the boat, he was doing two critically important things: trusting God and getting closer to him in the process. This is the essence of a Leap! We, as sinful humans, will sink every day—in the midst of our Leap and faith journey, we will be humbled on multiple occasions. We can live in that distant feeling from God—Adam and David and Peter sure did. Or we can come to grips with the fact that Leaping doesn't mean rainbows and butterflies off the bat, and God surely doesn't tell us to expect that either. What Leaping *does* accomplish is a more vulnerable position to trust him, rely on him, and see his greatness come to fruition in our lives.

And when you invite the Holy Spirit into your life, there's only one way forward: Leaping into uncertain waters.

CHAPTER 8

"Water is soft and humble, but it is the most powerful
and is the most endurable." —Debasish Mridha

In Chapter 5, I mentioned how the sense of control over the storm gives us comfort in areas that we cannot. The following is perhaps the greatest example in the Bible of someone who sought control and was given a slightly different task: loss of control on a quest to change the course of human history, forever.

Those last two sentences might bring Jesus of Nazareth to mind. When he prays "My Father, if it be possible, let this cup pass from me" while sweating blood in anxiety in the garden the night before his death, we see a human who made one last petition before the storm. But this chapter is not specifically about Jesus, or any event in the Gospel.

This is about a man who lived thousands of years before Jesus, but still prayed a similar prayer as Jesus that night.

So much of the church I grew up in focused on the New Testament. It's the introduction of Jesus, the Gospel, and the growth of the church. Most would agree, words throughout the New Testament provide more "relatable" aspects of Christianity today. However, in preparing to write this journey, I've spent more time in the Old Testament—specifically the journey of Moses and Joshua into the promised land. Reading Exodus through Joshua, in the middle of a global pandemic, will speak to anyone in ways unforeseen.

For the moment, let's scale back the idea from "Leaps" to mere "steps of faith." The Israelites in Egypt had many encounters of faith. From the plagues, where God tried to convince Pharaoh to let his people leave, to the Israelites following Moses' commands while listening to God. Eventually, we get to the Red Sea —a moment (in heavenly time) when God says "just trust me on this," and parts the Red Sea. This body of water was supposed to be a barrier, and actually served that purpose as a different kind of barrier to protect the Israelites. Upon first arrival, many Israelites must have sensed impending death—if God hadn't shown up in that moment, the reader certainly gets a dire sense of what could have happened.

Then God revealed His power and what occurred was miraculous. He parted the Red Sea for the Israelites, while the waves crashed down on the Egyptians trying to recapture them. All of this deliverance, only to lead them to the banks of the Jordan River—another body of water—with armies on the *opposite* side awaiting them. God had just shown up in a massive way, yet the people of God quickly lost their trust and admiration, so they turned back around to the safety of something in their control. It was a desert, but they felt a sense of control, probably even comfort too within the desert.

They had faced the water head on—feeling the wind of God part those waters, to shelter them on the frontend and protect them on the backend . . . yet it wasn't enough. The people didn't want to keep trusting in God. They didn't want to keep facing the adversity of faith . . . so for forty years they wandered. Do you have time to spend four decades waiting for God to show up?

So much time had already passed—between the events of Egyptian enslavement, crossing the Red Sea, and then the Jordan River. And before all that, there was a man who experienced smaller (but still significant) steps of faith. Moses experienced God through a burning bush, plagues in Egypt, and the Ten Commandments but would still not see the Promised Land. More on Moses in a little bit, but don't miss the *fear* and *lack of faith* that caused generations to pass on before true deliverance.

We press forward to Joshua, who was directed by God to tell the people of Israel: it is time to finally enter a new and Holy Land.

After Moses's death, Joshua gets to the banks of the Jordan River and is called to walk through it. Moments like these are where we wish God would part the sea (because we've seen Him do it before!) when in reality the journey through muck and mire is our calling.

The whole point of this section: God uses His creation of wind and water to cleanse us and help us feel His presence. In the Psalms, David talks about God being His shepherd and leading him beside quiet waters—refreshing to his soul. We can experience such peace and solitude in our lives because of the Good News of the Gospel. But that doesn't mean our lives will always be calm and comfortable.

We are still being called to take steps and leaps of faith. The water might be high and murky, and the wind may be trying to knock you off your feet, but there is a purpose and God is still with you. In Joshua 3, when the Israelites crossed into the promised land, the ark of the covenant was with them at all times. God, in the midst of the mud and water, had not left them—rather He was working at all times. What was later revealed to the Israelites is that the current stopped upstream (Joshua 3:13) once they stepped into the water. God *was* working for them, they just couldn't see it. All they saw was they were wet and muddy. This wasn't the same as crossing the Red Sea—but it was never supposed to be.

They needed to be washed in the mud so that they could see. Sound familiar?

It's the same miracle we see thousands of years later with Jesus—He used mud to help a blind man see for the first time (John 9).

The wind and the water—the grace of God and the Holy Spirit —is not specifically there to help you feel comfortable or in control. However the presence of those two realities mean you are not alone. You are never alone. God is not calling us to lead a life that satisfies *OUR* plan. He has made us for *His* purpose. Sometimes in the midst of our own journey, we get caught up in knowing that God loves us. And if He loves us, why would He lead us to such a dark place with no seemingly desirable outcome. In that thought process, we forget that God has been calling His people, for all of eternity, to a life of faith and following Him. To reach people that are stuck on their roof or with their house flooded. To step alongside the people in our lives who are stuck in the mud and can't see God.

It is comforting knowing that God loves us so much that He gave His only Son. Don't lose sight, however, that He loves all of us that much. His plan is to use you and the platform He gave you to reach others unto the ends of the earth.

The story we see unfold through Exodus and Joshua started with God calling one man to an uncomfortable path. How do we know that? Just look at this interaction from Exodus chapter four.

Moses: Oh, my Lord, I am not eloquent, either in the past or since you have spoken to your servant, but I am slow of speech and of tongue.

God: Who has made man's mouth? Who makes him mute, or deaf, or seeing, or blind? Is it not I, the Lord? Now therefore go, and I will be with your mouth and teach you what you shall speak.

Moses: Oh, my Lord, please send someone else.

Even when God tries to put Moses in his place, Moses *still* comes back with "send someone else."

In the year 2012, I felt a similar resistance and defiance toward God's plan. God had to humble me so much before I walked onto the football team at Louisville. When I didn't make the team the first time, I thought something similar to Moses: "Certainly this isn't meant for me, I was planning on playing baseball anyways."

In my wildest dreams and prayers, I couldn't have claimed what happened from 2012 to present day as my own. As I write this book, I am still active in the National Football League, yet I have been released six times in a (so far) four+ year career.

Our Leaps aren't perfect and don't always have soft landings. Our Leaps are opportunities to put full trust in God, stand in front of the water and walk. God will take care of the rest. There will be moments that we sink and possibly lose sight of our true purpose. Those moments feel like fog. Which leads me to God's answer to Moses—the final say in the matter that gave Moses confidence to walk through fog and approach the sea ahead.

God: Is there not Aaron, your brother, the Levite? I know that he can speak well. Behold, he is coming out to meet you, and when he sees you, he will be glad in his heart. You shall speak to him and put the words in his mouth, and I will be with your mouth and with his mouth and will teach you both what to do.

A helper. God sent Moses a friend, in the form of his brother, Aaron, to help him in the journey ahead.

COLIN HOLBA

Yet there was someone else.

Shortly after God's words about Aaron, in Exodus 4, we read about a circumcision story like no other.

"At a lodging place on the way the Lord met him and sought to put him to death. Then Zipporah took a flint and cut off her son's foreskin and touched Moses' feet with it and said, "Surely you are a bridegroom of blood to me!" So he let him alone. It was then that she said, "A bridegroom of blood," because of the circumcision." —*Exodus 4:24-26*

A brief paraphrase: God sought to put Moses to death. Zipporah, acting swiftly, circumcises their son (a sign of God's chosen people), and God spares Moses for it.

We don't see a lot of Zipporah in and through Exodus, but it doesn't take but a few sentences to realize Moses could not have completed his call without her. A knucklehead given a giant task—amid his reluctance to accept the work, a woman saved his life so that he could continue said work.

Needless to say, I can relate to Moses.

This is the point in the book where we recognize something incredibly important: you are not alone. Are we with God? Of course He is always by your side. But as you encounter the storm, take a second to listen. Who has He given to help you encounter the storm?

With Moses, he sent Aaron. And wouldn't you know it, he did

LEAP!

the same for me.

PART 3

CHAPTER 9

"Pain doesn't tell you when you ought to stop. Pain is the little voice in your head that tries to hold you back because it knows if you continue you will change." —*Kobe Bryant*

In Chapter 2, I briefly mentioned a good friend of mine, Aaron Nance. In a similar way to how I mentioned him and moved on—we often experience miracles in our lives from God before moving on just as quickly.

Aaron Nance and his influence on my life is a miracle. I'm sure you have an Aaron in your life, and if you don't already, I pray one day you're lucky enough to identify such an impactful person as part of your story.

Before my *own* words on why our relationship has meant so much to me, and how his influence contributed to multiple Leaps in my life, I wanted to add his own personal touch to this book and journey. That's right—for the next few paragraphs, you get a much needed break from Colin Holba. I hope Aaron's words give you perspective of how God speaks through individuals and how when the paths of believers cross, there is opportunity for a miracle to take place—even if you skim over the miracle and its importance the first time.

Here is Aaron in his own words:

When I was in high school, one of my early prayers was that I would have a family that looked like God's Kingdom. While my prayer did

LEAP!

not use those exact words, that was the concept I hoped for. You see, I did not come from a two-parent home—my mom and dad were not together but I would see my dad every other weekend. So early on I knew my situation was not ideal, but I did not understand why. Life went on and I didn't think much of that prayer. Growing up, I knew a family was not in my near-future, so I focused on athletics. Athletics led me to the University of Louisville where I tried out for the football team after a fairly successful high school career.

While I never received an athletic scholarship at Louisville, I made the team and thought it would at least get me onto the field. It was not common for "walk-ons" to play but I knew all I needed was an opportunity. That opportunity came during the fourth game of my freshman season when we traveled to Arkansas State. After that game, I was as confident as ever. I was a freshman, I was a walk-on, I had just played in my first collegiate game, and I knew that MY future was bright. As the season went on, I played in every game before Louisville solidified a spot in the Beef 'O' Brady's Bowl. As we prepared for the bowl game, I knew this would be a great opportunity to catapult my growth as we headed into the offseason.

During one of our bowl game practices, we were doing a screen drill —just a little dump-off pass to me in the flat. I caught the ball, made a move, and I went knee to knee with a defender. As painful as that was, I knew that opportunities could be taken as quickly as they were given. So, I decided to push through the pain even though my knee felt unstable. My very next play I caught the ball, made the same move and felt my knee buckle. That one play started a cycle in my college football career. I tore my ACL. Over the next two seasons, I would tear my knee up two more times. The knee injuries were significant because they led me to a place where I would eventually find peace. In order to deal with the mental and emotional pain of no longer being able to play, I went to the basketball gym and just shot the ball. This was not an easy task, seeing how my leg was in a brace most of the time when I went to the gym. I couldn't move so all I could do was stand in front of the rim and work on my shooting form. Of course, I would complete my football workouts but I didn't want to be there. I found solace shooting a basketball.

This quickly became my reality for the next three years. Each year my jump shot got a little better. It is important to note I've always had a love for basketball, but I chose to play football because I did not think playing basketball on a collegiate level was in the cards for me. This insecurity dates back to childhood days but that's another story for another book. I had no clue at the time, but God was going to use the very thing that once caused me defeat to change the trajectory of my life.

While dealing with the issues of injury and going through a major identity crisis, a young lady came into my life by the name Margret Harris. I knew early on I wanted her to be my wife but then I began to think about the dynamics of my family. What once looked like it could be special eventually turned into heartache, so my prayer resurfaced:

"God show me what it looks like to be a Kingdom husband and a Kingdom father."

I wanted to be everything that Margret dreamed of, but I didn't know how to get there. I was so used to memorizing playbooks and having coaches tell me how to get better and move onto the next level, so it only seemed right to have some sort of resource for the most important team I'd ever play on: my family.

After some time had passed, Margret and I started dating, and it eventually led to an engagement and then marriage. During the process, I was playing more and more basketball. My knee felt great and I had started making a little name for myself in the city of Louisville. Some people took notice, and I was invited to play in a pro-am basketball League. My performance in that league landed me an opportunity to play overseas. I had to make a decision within a week. Long story short, I declined the offer because Margret and I knew we were ready to start a family, and we just didn't feel comfortable with that kind of a life change. She likely wouldn't have accompanied me for a while, and to accept the offer would have meant a long-distance relationship for several months—we weren't even a year into our marriage. It was a tough decision, but it was also effortless knowing my biggest cheerleader wouldn't be in the stands. I also knew that being away for seven months was not how I wanted to start my marriage. So, Margret and I prayed together that if it is something God had for us then the opportunity would come around again, but this time my wife would be there with me.

Fast forward about a year later and we were introduced to an agent with some connections to the NBA. In my head I was thinking, "Why not?"

Margret and I were a year-and-a-half into our marriage, and just found out we were pregnant with our first child. In addition, I had a job teaching and coaching in the city. So, leaving job security for a pipe dream made absolutely no sense. NONE! Let's pause and bring this thing half circle—you'll see the full connections a bit later. I went to college to play football, tore up my knee, started shooting in the gym just to cope, played in the pro-am league, got an offer to play overseas, then received a request (per my agent) to take my family to another state (Dallas, TX) for training and very little job security. It all makes no sense on paper. Thank you for following. Here's the rest of the story.

We ended up moving to Dallas at the encouragement of, again, my biggest cheerleader, Margret. While in Dallas, I connected with a man named Jonathan Pitts and his wife, Wynter. Jonathan and Wynter had known my wife for some time because Margret lived in Texas before going to school at UofL and spent most summers with them when she would go home for breaks. They had become mentors to Margret. Jonathan and Wynter had four girls and their focus was to lead their family the way God had intended. The Pitts opened their home for Margret and me to stay while I pursued this dream of basketball.

My schedule in that season was nothing short of unconventional. I would wake up early to see Jonathan praying over his girls before they went to school. I would go workout and come back to the house where I would see Jonathan reading his Bible. At the time I didn't think much of it. I would go workout again and at dinner I would see Jonathan leading his family in devotion.

Not only did I see this side of Jonathan being a Kingdom father, but I was also able to see Jonathan and Wynter and their Kingdom marriage.

It started to click: this man was intentional about leading his family. Those opportunities don't just happen every day by chance— such a lifestyle creates moments of deep engagement. I knew the mindset Jonathan had is what I was missing. I needed to see that. Watching them lead their family was something I was not used to, but it looked right. Now, when God says He's going to do something, He likes to flex a little bit for His children. Not only was I able to see Jonathan and Wynter's marriage but I was also able to see the marriage of another man named Jonathan (Evans) and his wife, Kanika. The way these men love their wives and their children amazes me to this day, and I knew I wanted that for my life. They took pride in leading their family. God could have stopped there but He said, "I'm not done yet, I have one more for you." Not only were we being influenced by the Pitts family and the Evans family, but I was also being influenced by the union of Dr. Tony and Mrs. Lois Evans. Dr. Evans is the father of Jonathan Evans and the uncle of Wynter Pitts.

In high school, I prayed a prayer that I revisited in college and it did not come to pass until after I was married. When I look back over my life, I realize that God strategically allowed certain things to happen to move me in a direction and prepare me for his Kingdom purpose and an answered prayer. Time to bring this thing full circle. If I would have never chosen to play football (my original Leap!), I would have never gotten hurt. And if I never had gotten hurt, I would have never gone to the gym to work on my jump shot. If I had never worked on my jump shot, I would never have had the opportunity to go to Texas and if I never had the opportunity to go to Texas, I would have never seen God answer my prayer in seeing what a Kingdom family looked like.

The entire time God was working on something that I could not see but after I moved in the direction, I felt like he was calling me to, everything started to make sense. A lot of times God will not show you what He is doing until after you Leap and trust him. As long as you're holding on to human reason and understanding you will never see God move in your life. It made no sense for me to quit my job with benefits, pack up my pregnant wife, move three states away to pursue a dream of basketball. Now I realize basketball was not the reason for me going to Dallas TX, but it was the tool to get me to where God needed me to develop me for my destiny.

The beauty of God's miracles in our lives, to me, is that we are all on different paths with different platforms and time frames, but we are all called to do the same thing. Aaron Nance is one of

LEAP!

the most influential people in my life—not only as it relates to my football journey, but for this book as a whole. The courage he took in his own Leaps, yes, but also his mentorship and faithfulness as a husband, father, friend, athlete, and leader.

To be very honest with you, I can't tell you exactly how we got there, but one day I found myself eating breakfast in the Louisville student center with Aaron.

In the fall of 2012, every Monday and Wednesday at 9am before my next class, Aaron and I had breakfast. I felt comfortable approaching him because I went to an FCA meeting one time during my freshman year. For about eight weeks straight, we never missed breakfast. I started to grow closer in my walk with God as I spent more time with Aaron. I found myself drawing closer to God's Word and could see tangible growth in my faith—simply from being around a man striving to know God.

Aaron might be the best athlete you have never heard about. He was not undersized out of high school, but he was under-recruited. He never lacked talent, but coaches lacked faith in him for some reason. Nance went to UofL as an under-recruited and under-valued walk-on at wide receiver. Size, speed and athleticism were all he had—that's what God had given him. His idea of collegiate success, at first, was significant playing time, quality statistics, and earning a scholarship. All of the things talented walk-ons desire.

That just wasn't the platform God had for him.

Three ACL surgeries into college and he realized the plan he had

89

in mind wasn't God's plan. But you read his story—Nance was faithful, and his journey ultimately wasn't about the impact he could make on the football field or basketball court.

God brought him back to UofL for the impact that he could make off the field—not just me in our time as students together, but alongside all of the people that he has interacted with on campus.

His ACL injuries as a student gave him time to grow acquainted with the Fellowship of Christian Athletes. Serving at UofL helped him become a teacher and high school football coach—two massive platforms that God can use in amazing ways.

Most pointedly, as it relates to my story, Nance was the one who really helped me make the football team at UofL. His role as a student coach, while he was working through his ACL injuries, is why he was at my first try out for the football team. So even when I literally fell down in an agility drill, I knew I had someone in my corner. When I had to wait two more months before trying out again, I had someone who could give me insight to what the coaches wanted to see. The miracles of God are so much more than the human mind can comprehend. While God was preparing me for the platform, he was active with the platforms for others around me—very similar to the story of Moses and Aaron in the bible.

I can't imagine the pain and frustration during Nance's humbling journey.

I talk about hard work, but hard work in college, for me, looked like showing up and remaining faithful to the Holy Spirit's direction. Where the wind blew my kite, I'd go.

The earthly platform that he was striving to gain success on crumbled. However God makes no mistakes, He takes no missteps. Nance's prayer was to be a kingdom husband, a kingdom father. That was the prayer that God was answering, that was the platform that God was working on. I don't know if Nance ever knew even the influence that he had not only on me, but everyone around him in college. His faithfulness didn't go unnoticed. His impact, I know, stretches far beyond his own understanding. He was exactly where God needed him, to grow his platform.

Aaron may never realize the impact he has had on me. Specifically, the way I lead as a Christian, mentor, husband, and father. His prayers of athletic success were stifled, because I am sure that he never prayed or worked for the results that he got. I'm not sure if he prayed for God to use him and advance his kingdom in whatever way he saw fit. I'm not sure if he asked God to give him a platform to be able to impact the kingdom in a positive way. But if he didn't I'm fairly confident others prayed on his behalf, because those prayers were answered!

"And we know that in all things God works for the good of those who love him, who have been called according to his purpose." —Romans 8:28

Is our purpose to be great at sports, excel in business, or to advance His kingdom? Ultimately, God has called us all to the same purpose: to humbly serve Him all of our days on earth. He will interweave beautiful miracles at the perfect time. Our stories and the stories of those around us will bring glory to Him. Because the more we communicate and converse with God, the more we understand one of the most important realities of all: God doesn't make mistakes.

He didn't with Moses. He didn't with Aaron. And He won't with you, either.

CHAPTER 10

"Good communication is just as stimulating as black coffee, and just as hard to sleep after." —Anne Morrow Lindbergh

The most intriguing content I consume has a common thread: it feels natural. Whether it is a blog post, news article, video clip, podcast or book, the media that is most captivating to me feels like I am sitting in on a conversation. Some of the best sermons I've listened to, there is a focus not on *preaching* but of talking with the church. Those are the moments I feel like someone is talking directly to me. The best podcasts I listen to are fantastic conversations that draw the listener close and make them feel like they're a part of it.

My bible study group once worked through *Every Good Endeavor* by Tim Keller. In the book's introduction, Keller recounts a story from J.R.R. Tolkien called *Leaf by Niggle*. I was completely enthralled by Niggle's story. Tolkien was such a gifted communicator—whether through *Lord of the Rings* or *Leaf by Niggle*, he wrote in a natural way that made you forget about the world around you. Even Keller, who just gives a synopsis of this story, writes in a natural, comfortable, and relatable way that I could see myself as Niggle (the protagonist).

93

Niggle was a friend, neighbor, and artist who was commissioned to go on a journey. However, his whole life was consumed with making a painting. He would spend hours on this painting, trying to make every leaf, on every tree, perfect. But there was something disrupting his work on the painting—he would reluctantly help his neighbor, Parish.

Niggle spent his entire time obsessing over the painting that was in front of him, yet never felt like he could complete it. It wasn't until long after his journey that Niggle was able to see one single leaf be displayed. He had spent so much time trying to create the perfect masterpiece, and yet, one leaf was the influence that was displayed for the entire town to see. He was so involved with what was pressing on his heart and his mind, he didn't have time to communicate with Parish, with himself, or even with God.

Like Niggle, I've hit roadblocks in this life. But the determining factor, in each of those moments, is the extent of my communication with God—or lack thereof. The times I am confident in my walk with God, I know I can push through distractions and roadblocks to complete the work God gave me. Even if the work is something as simple as painting a leaf, the mission is to walk alongside my neighbor on the journey before me.

To my knowledge, the idea of *how* we communicate with God isn't a hot topic of discussion. As I grew into adulthood, my experience with *how* I talk to God mostly centered around prayer. That's not to say I wasn't taught *about* prayer, but just that it was the only medium on how I was taught to talk to God. In addition, it was the most direct way to hear God. I was told to get into the Word, read my Bible, pray, and pray some more. For the record, I think all of those options are a great place to start.

Reading your bible is the most direct way you can consume the word of God—literally, it is "God breathed" (2 Timothy 3:16-17).

For me, in my faith journey, prayer from my heart has always been a little bit like jazz—improvised and off the cuff. For my wife, Lauren, however, she grew up experiencing prayer in a more premeditated sense. Whether that be liturgy or singing on Sunday morning. Early on in our relationship, that was a little intimidating to me.

Intimidating not only because the written prayers are beautiful and majestic, but also because it made me ask questions like "How *should* we approach the Lord of the Universe? Rehearsed or not?"

For years, prayer felt like checking a box before eating a meal, going to bed, or something big in life happening. Throw up a hail Mary prayer, wait to see immediately what happens, generally if it goes the way I want it to, forget to thank the God I just prayed to, and so on. Prayer growing up wasn't a thing I did to truly try and connect or communicate with God. For a good portion of my adolescent years, my vocal communication really wasn't even that good. It wasn't until I wrote things down and took time to explain all of the thoughts that were rushing to my head that I learned how to communicate more effectively. To go back to the start of this chapter, my communication with God started to feel natural.

When I started writing down my thoughts, and reading them, hearing them and praying them is when I could *feel* the weight of those prayers. My communication with God changed when I started processing my testimony—verbal or written—of where I used to be, where I was at currently and where I wanted to go with the Lord. It was in those moments God would speak to me in a way that I could hear Him.

In all of my years praying, I can't remember hearing His audible voice or feeling His physical presence. In addition, writing my prayers is what led me to read my bible more. My heart started leading me there. I started to experience joy and excitement while developing thoughts and connections—this was how God was and still communicates with me. Writing and waiting, sometimes weeks at a time, as pages fill with things only the Lord could have revealed. This is how my communication with God has developed over time, and they are at their most intense when I sense a Leap out of my comfort zone on the horizon. I see God in the small things, and a few times throughout the week make a point to write them down—then I watch those small things unfold generally in ways that would go unnoticed, if not noted earlier, yet in the small, mundane, you can see miracles.

Still there are more ways.

Some of the moments that mean the most, when I can really *feel* God speaking to me, are in conversations with others. Generally, these moments are unsuspecting. Then you get chills or the back of your neck starts to tingle. There's a brief thought of "This is bigger than me and I don't know why." These are the times to practice taking the Leap! God is stirring up something in you, to say, and most likely to hear, that is specific for that moment in time. Lean into those moments—become vulnerable with yourself and the person on the other end of the conversation. I haven't seen any burning bushes in my lifetime, but I have felt the flame of the Lord speaking to me when I let the wind lead me deeper into a conversation that feels Spirit-led.

Communication is crucial in taking a Leap. In other words, the way you communicate or talk to yourself is vital in any big decision process. I don't like the phrase "self talk" because it often carries a negative connotation. I'd rather see it as communicating with yourself—just like how we've described communicating with God. Maybe you similarly start to view "self talk" in a positive light by journaling and processing decisions in your own life.

Our team chaplain at UofL, Chris Morgan, used to say "If someone can convince you into something, then somebody else can convince you out of it."

I think that this is so true—especially if an idea is playing on your feelings and emotions. You could hear something in one mindset or if the emotions are set right, but once the scene or environment changes your thoughts and heart could change as well. The same thing can be said if you are just trying to tell yourself something—especially if it's not the way you communicate best with yourself.

Write things down. I know it sounds repetitive to what I just talked about, but it's the truth. If I have a list of things I want to get done the next day, I don't make a giant laundry list of things, but I do write down two or three things that are important. When I want to continually keep myself on track, I write it on the mirror—to see and digest as much as I can. This works for me.

Learning how you process things or how you think things through has to be one of the first things you do before stepping out on a ledge. Especially if you have a spouse or someone who is deeply connected to you.

In one instance, during my freshman year of college, I remember God speaking to me through the truth in Philippians 1:12.

"Now I want you to know, brothers and sisters, that what has happened to me has actually served to advance the gospel."

I had just tried out for the football team for the first time, and found out I didn't make the team. For a few hours between finding out I hadn't made the team, and reading this passage. I really wasn't as frustrated and upset as I thought I should be. There was this sense, that this was a path, forged on heavenly time, and I just needed to continue to prepare on my end, waiting for God's timing.

After reading that passage, I knew it didn't matter if I ever ended up making the football team or continued to wash laundry for the baseball team. God would use me to advance the Gospel as long as I was faithful and remained in communication with Him while continuing to learn myself—how I learned new information and could communicate with others. The rest of my college ride was pretty wild, but my only hope is that through some of it I was able to advance the Gospel like Paul told the church at Philippi.

He wrote those words down to help them process a call to action. And I encourage you to write yours down as well—you never know what those words might lead to. But I hope they bring you closer to God no matter where His plan leads.

CHAPTER 11

"I alone cannot change the world, but I can cast a stone across the waters to create many ripples." – Mother Teresa

I talked about our team chaplain, Chris Morgan. Chris entered his time at UofL through an organization called Fellowship of Christian Athletes (FCA). You might have heard of FCA before as they come alongside athletes and teams all across the country to remind others of why anyone plays the game: to glorify God with the ability they've been given.

The work he has done to steward and proclaim the Gospel, not only in my life, but in the lives of others is immeasurable. His ministry at FCA started in 2006 with just six athletes who attended his meetings on a regular basis. By my freshman year in 2012, those meetings had grown to about 50 recurring attendees—a massive jump in itself. As of 2021, even after a global pandemic that changed on-campus events entirely, it has grown to a weekly attendance of over 400 college athletes.

LEAP!

With that said, Chris always redirects praise—pointing back to The Lord with some help from Chick-fil-A. (Get a free Chick-fil-A sandwich at every Monday night event). From 2012 to now, the discipleship aspect through FCA leaves a ripple effect long after any athlete hangs up the cleats. It's a true "X-Factor" that sets FCA apart: the longevity of impact that stems from participating even if only for a season of life.

After I made the football team I started to interact more with FCA, I was able to sit down and talk to Chris. I was able to share my story with him and where I was—about my mindset when I came to college and what my mindset was now that I was on the football team (circa March 2013). He asked me about my faith, what that journey looked like growing up, and what that looked like since being on my own in college.

I told him my story. I remember thinking, at that point, God had taken me a pretty long way. He asked me to share my testimony with the entire FCA on a Monday night. No longer was I being asked to sit in the back and quietly eat free chicken—he wanted me to open up in front of everybody. To show the entire room what I had been trying to hide and keep covered for years. This wasn't something new to FCA and their discipleship model, but it was new to me and a call to action that was hard for me to process.

The "X-Factor" I just mentioned started with sitting down, writing a personal testimony, and then sharing it. That's it. It doesn't seem like much, but since then I've become such an open book (no pun intended). Sharing my story is just part of who I am now. Every Monday before any FCA, a different student athlete or former athlete would get on stage and share their story. They shared where they were and what God had done in their life. Great or small, every story was genuine, unique, and empowering. It was one thing to hear Chris open up and share about his time as an athlete, husband, and father. But that was his job after all—to share those things on a consistent basis, and then give a good sermon.

That's what I thought at the time, yet I had no idea the impact of sharing your story with others or what that looks like.

I remember being so nervous—shaking and sweating . . . word of advice, stay away from grey shirts if you're nervous speaking in front of people.

I had given two other public speeches before that instance, and both went well. One for a senior class president and the other for a public speaking class—but nothing like this. In my head I felt naked and exposed in front of all my peers. The huge shot of confidence I received a few months before, after making the football team, was gone. I didn't feel qualified to stand in front of those people and heck . . . I was still just a nobody, tackling dummy, walk-on long snapper.

In my head, I liked the idea of the platform in class. In class, I was an athlete. I had a team, and some status on campus. At FCA, I was surrounded by future first round picks, olympic gold medalists and many more accomplished, or going to be accomplished athletes. That was the thing though, my testimony wasn't about how I earned a spot on a sports team at UofL, and it certainly wasn't about the importance of my position on that team. Rather it was about how I embraced the role of Christ in my life, how I became a member of His team, and the impact that identity has in my life. It was in those moments, I didn't find significance, but I found courage. I was on a stage to talk about the role God had and was having in my life, not to shallowly talk about my athletic gifts that got me to where I was, because truly, I was still terribly unathletic in comparison to that room.

I think that is the perfect metaphor. Oftentimes we want to share about the significance of our worldly roles and try to impress that on people. In reality, God can use anyone at any moment in any role, He just needs to have someone willing to proclaim the impact He has had on them, and what it means to be a part of His team.

There I was. And now here I am—sharing my story on paper with who knows how many people.

Spend some time after you finish this book thinking about where God has taken you. Even if you don't think it's very far, be your own radio host next time you are in the shower and talk through your story. God hasn't given us our testimony to keep to ourselves. He hasn't placed people in our lives for us to not share the impact that they have had on us. Start with the people who have had an impact on you. Share with them the impact they have had in your life. Reflect on when someone came into your life and the purpose that was behind it, even if they were gone when you realized that purpose.

Every Monday after I shared that night, I'd go back to eat more Chick-fil-A and hear more incredible testimonies. That was nearly five years of my life, and it had an immense impact on me. Even if you can't bear to share it, write down your testimony. (More on this in a little bit). Write down your journey and reflect on the moments that happened that have led you to where you are right now. I'm sure even in those stories, maybe without even realizing it, there were moments that you even took Leaps of faith too.

And don't lose what you've written. There are few things as powerful as your own words in writing. As the reassurance you are giving yourself that not only has God provided for me, but this is the exact way He did it. Even when I couldn't understand what was happening, He was working for me, and now I can see it plain as day. Just as Joshua and the Isrealites were in the mud, it didn't mean that they were alone.

I didn't want to just fill this book with my story or Aaron Nance's. I have always wanted to hear from others outside of FCA or my own little bubble. To hear and maybe share their story, testimony and Leap. Soon, you'll read a couple Leap stories from two of my friends that also had an immense impact on me—I asked them to write and share their own story, and I hope you glean something strong from how God has worked in their lives. Examples of just how powerful and holy and big God is—even when we don't feel or see it in the moment.

One of the stories you'll read is about Cliff Marshall—a strength coach at UofL.

Cliff reached out to me to help me train mentally and physically—not just as a client, but as a brother in Christ. He didn't need me as an athlete. He was doing fine in that department. But for the one time a week we worked together, he poured into me as if I was purposefully placed in his life.

Another story you'll read is of Shilo Becker—my good friend in a foreign land. My time with the San Francisco 49ers was the greatest mental test I have experienced thus far as a professional. The emotional path I was on of being alone and far away from home was a lot to bear. Shilo had no reason to be the friend to me that she was. I easily could have just been another face in the hotel. Yet she walked with me in that season—always helping Lauren and I work through the transition of life apart. I became friends with her and her boyfriend and shared meals, conversations and life with them. To this day, we share Christmas cards and support each and our families from thousands of miles away. My wife, who has never met her in person, feels like she knows her as a close friend.

These are people, for reasons only known to God, who were placed in my life for a brief season, but our friendships are still alive and active. I asked them to share their stories in this book and they jumped at the opportunity. I want to show you this book is not just about me and my story or my Leap(s) in life. It's not about Aaron Nance or Chris Morgan or even my beautiful wife, Lauren. It's about how God uses all of us for very specific reasons and He wants us to share His story—a story that uses us as its main characters.

Recently, I had a conversation with another pro athlete at a local gym. He knew I was a Christian—he had not faced the smoothest road of being a pro athlete. I asked him, "What does life after baseball look like for you?"

Being that it was at the gym he didn't go into too much detail. I could tell, though, that he had spent some serious time thinking about it. He set up parameters for continuing the grind for baseball, but was prepared for what life afterwards would be like.

I asked him this question because, while not dealing with the same struggles in baseball as I had in football, I had finally not been defensive about that question and was now curious to see what other people had thought about. In years past, when my phone wasn't ringing my wife would ask me the similar question:

"What do you want to do after football, Colin?"

Early on I would immediately get defensive and become rude.

"Do you not have faith in me that I can do this?" I'd think to myself, "Do you not think I can finally make it? Look, football hasn't been perfect but it has provided thus far."

Those statements are so elementary, but in my heart that was where my heart was at that time.

My beautiful, loving, and supportive wife just asked me good questions about life, and I was a snake in response. It wasn't until I started writing this book that two things happened.

1) I could finally answer what I was passionate about and 2) truly apologize to her for reacting poorly in those moments.

Suffice to say, it took a while for me to be able to admit to myself that I was insecure about my football career—the words Carson spoke in the forward couldn't be more spot on:

"Football is what you do, it's not who you are."

I projected other people as having a lack of faith in me, because I felt like I was letting myself down, and worse yet—letting my wife down. And for as many good friends who have supported me in a parakletos manner (we're going Greek in Chapter 12), it is my closest friend, Lauren, who pivoted from medical school to nursing school for my football career. She has trusted me throughout this journey and just wants better insight into my mind. She asked questions I wasn't ready to ask myself.

When you find those people in your life, and if you're lucky enough to find it in a spouse, then you'll finally realize one of the most important aspects about taking a Leap:

We weren't meant to jump alone.

CHAPTER 12

"You can take skydiving lessons, study aerodynamics, learn how to fold a parachute, and enter an airplane. You can put on a helmet and a parachute and stand at the door, but you still won't know what skydiving is like. There comes a point when you have to jump." —Fr. Dwight Longenecker

Something else Chris Morgan would always say—It wasn't his original quote, but boy am I glad he repeated it and hammered it into my mind: "If you want to go fast, go alone, if you want to go far, go together."

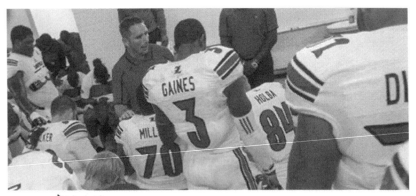

UofL FCA

Time and time again he would reference that quote. From speaking about Godly relationships to pregame pep-talks in the hotel before a game. No matter the setting, the message was the same: we *can* get things done by ourselves, but God didn't create us to be in solitude—we were formed in His image which is an image of community and unity. The aspect of a team is so special. Within a team setting, you can have a defined role that you specialize in. Communities that worked together historically were able to advance quickly because of specialization.

Teams also create a support system unlike any other.

You don't have to be your very best, at all times, every second of the day. There are people on your team, in solidarity *with* you, to obtain any common goal. When you are too tired to go, they have your back. When you don't trust yourself, they infuse confidence in you. When you doubt your purpose, they are there to encourage you, fight the good fight and continue as one.

The idea of teams also brings about accountability greater than yourself. You can't let the people down beside you, because you

LEAP!

are all on a mission together. I have to think that when God was creating His "chosen people" this is why He decided on the 12 tribes of Israel. When Jesus was calling his disciples, He called 12 and when Paul traveled to the early church, he was with Barnabas, John Mark and Timothy. We've already mentioned how Moses wasn't alone—he had his wife, Zipporah, and brother, Aaron, and eventually Joshua.

This is the God of all humanity, and examples of community don't just line up with the Bible.

Michael Jordan had Scottie Pippen. Tom Brady had Gronk, Edelman, and of course, Belichick. Young and Montana had not only Jerry Rice, but Bill Walsh. Even individual athletes and all of their accomplishments—you rarely hear Serena Williams talk about her success without mentioning Venus or their father. Same with Tiger Woods and his Dad and swing coach. Same with authors like Tolkien and Lewis who had The Inklings. The examples go on and on, and they will forever because that is how God created us. We were not created to go about life on our own.

COLIN HOLBA

Parakletos is a Greek word.

Most often used in Jewish texts during the Roman and Byzantine Empires, the word is derived from two traditional Greek words: "para" and "kletos." Even today we use the prefix "para" for a multitude of words: paramilitary, paralegal, parallel, and even parachute. "Para" is defined as a Greek prefix with many meanings—most definitions include "alongside of," "beside, near, and resembling." Think about paramilitary which means to work beside the military. Or the same is said for paralegal—alongside legal professionals. Parallel means two lines running alongside each other. Even the word "parachute" which at first glance doesn't follow too much with the previous words, but with a little further look makes perfect sense.

We've just mentioned how "para" means "alongside." Well, "chute" on the other hand was borrowed from a French word. "Chute" comes from the word "cheoir" in old French or "cadere" in Latin—both of which mean "to fall."

Word study may seem like a bit of a tangent, but essentially, in a more historic and traditional sense of the word, parachute means more than just what Dictionary.com will tell you. What the word really means is "beside your fall."

What about "kletos"? This word on its own means "called or invited." This is not a word that we are as familiar with in English. Kletos is more foreign to us, and is more of a word that we might hear a pastor say and not recognize. You probably

LEAP!

couldn't even impress your Greek friends with it, because it is a term almost strictly used in Jewish/Greek texts.

Now, think for a moment about the "red letters" in many bibles that Jesus Himself said—things He himself has been historically recorded saying.

"Parakletos" is one of those words.

That is why this word is important. Yes, Jesus spoke it, but more importantly he knew its significance. Most commonly, we see Jesus in the Gospel of John talk about an "Advocate" or a "Helper" which we translate in a couple different ways. But in Greek, this is one in the same word. Parakletos therefore means, in an unofficial Colin Holba definition, "Called alongside" or more officially, "One who is invited beside."

In Part One of this book, I talked about a sermon from Lead Pastor at Southeast Christian Church, Kyle Idleman. I summarize John in that section saying that Jesus even told His disciples that someone better was coming.

The actual verses referenced were John 16:12-13: *"I have much more to say to you, more than you can now bear. But when he, the Spirit of truth, comes, he will guide you into all the truth. He will not speak on his own; he will speak only what he hears, and he will tell you what is yet to come."*

As Jesus talks to His disciples before He ascends to Heaven, He doesn't quite use the vernacular "Holy Spirit" to his disciples.

What word did he use? You guessed it: Parakletos.

113

At the time, His disciples would have known what the *word* meant, but they did not know what *Jesus* meant. They thought of Advocate or Helper. Even some of your translations intertwine those names with the Holy Spirit. They didn't know who "He" was. They were just told to be patient. More importantly, that He was going to be the voice of God to them. In the very next verse, John 16:14: *"He will glorify me because it is from me that he will receive what he will make known to you."*

Read it again, but read it this way, "The one who is invited beside will glorify me because it is from me what he will make known to you."

Even in our worship of Jesus, we are created to do so in company— in the presence of "the one who is invited alongside."

I've mentioned how the idea of becoming a father has changed my perspective. For those of you who are parents, this hits home. For those of you who are yet to be parents, it will. The moment your partner tells you that you're going to be a parent, it won't sink in immediately, but it will flip a switch that you didn't know existed. More importantly, God created my wife, Lauren, to be my partner and vice versa—to be the person I do life with. Life with her started at age 22, and with our oath to each other and God, it will be until the air ceases to fill our lungs that we are together.

We are created to do this life and journey as part of a community—think of that word broken into its two parts, "common unity."

I am so thankful that God created Lauren, in His own image, for us to do life together, forever. God didn't just create your spouse to be your community. Aaron Nance and Chris Morgan are some of the best mentors I have ever had, and they have shared that role not only for me, but for so many other athletes at UofL.

Just as God gave Moses his closest community. And just as Jesus had the 12. Just as Paul had Timothy, you will have people throughout life that will fill your cup. They will grow with you and support you. They will share a common unity throughout your life. Not everyone is meant to be in our lives forever, but each and everyone of us was created for a purpose. Some of those purposes are for a fleeting moment, with their impact serving only a short time, but their influence changes the trajectory of your life.

I want to swing back to Parakletos for a moment.

It is one of the most important things, in my opinion, that Jesus ever said. Yes, there was the Sermon on the Mount which was monumentally important. But Parakletos is different from Immanuel, God with us—this funny word means God invited to be with us, forever. To be an advocate for the throne and a compass for our life. In moments we are trying to determine Leaps of faith and where they will go, what will happen next?

God didn't leave us to take that Leap by ourselves.

On earth, He gives us mentors, friends, pastors, and maybe a spouse. He provides the team you need to cultivate the courage to continuously take Leaps. He doesn't leave us there. Just as the kite needs wind to catch flight, The Lord has left you with something else: The Advocate, The Helper, and the Parachute "beside your fall." Your advocate is a parachute, and the wind will catch your chute, it will guide you to safety.

I have never skydived. I'm sure it would be many flights for me to jump if it is anything like my mindset for a diving board. But I can imagine you don't get on that plane for the ride. You don't get on that plane to see the Earth from that vantage point—there are far more secure ways to do that. You don't get on that plane for any reason other than to jump. You also don't get on that plane without a team around you—a pilot to take you off the ground, experienced divers to guide you along your journey, and your parachute. The true reason you have confidence to take that Leap is because the parachute will catch you. There is faith, not only that the instructor will help you enjoy the experience of a lifetime, but the parachute will catch you and safely bring you to your destination.

You do not Leap alone. Not from a plane 10,000 feet above the ground, nor with your life firmly on the ground.

"If you want to go fast, go alone, but if you want to go far, go together."

We are specifically designed to go far—to go farther than our own imagination could ever take us. Never in my wildest dreams did I think, when I walked into my locker room as a high school junior to tell my coach I was quitting football, that I would ever play again. And then God introduced Kyle Todd and Aaron Nance, and slowly but surely my team was built, and I gained trust in my parachute. Never did I think in 2010 that I would ever play football again, and then in 2017 I received a phone call from Mike Tomlin telling me that the Steelers were picking me in the 6th round to be on their team. Or at the end of 2020, while battling identity issues and a depressed state of mind, that God would speak to me through writing a book.

To go farther together is not simply a parable for the tortoise and the hare—this is a calling by God. The calling is one we are meant to find for ourselves and help others find in the process. God does not call us for speed or earthly success—rather, He calls us to exalt Him.

That all of what we do is worship Him.

I can't think of anything better than a community growing together, finding and embracing their platforms and encouraging everyone to take their Leap. Your teammates may not be in your life to jump with you, but they may be there to help you get on the plane. Others *will* be there in the plane and some on the ground—some may be at the next jump site, but you are never alone . . . you were created for community.

You were created to do things that are bigger than yourself.

How can we glorify God while still on the plane? You have been given a parachute and you have a team around you. If reading through this book wasn't evidence enough: I'm now a part of your team.

COLIN HOLBA

How will you ever feel the power of God while you're standing on the ground, or holding onto the handle?

You are called to action, you were designed with a purpose, and it's time to take your Leap!

PART 4

TAKE YOUR LEAP

"Nothing diminishes anxiety faster than action."
—Walter Anderson

To me, there's no such thing as coincidence in our lives.

As sort of a recap of my Leap story—much of which was covered in this book—here is a list I can in no way chalk up to mere coincidence:

- I quit football after my junior year of high school.
- Was an equipment manager on UofL's baseball team my freshman year.
- Met Aaron Nance and felt compelled to take a Leap: to walk onto the football team for my sophomore season.
- Tried out once and didn't make it.
- Tried out again and made the team.
- Got a new coaching staff and was put on scholarship.
- Was a two year starter.
- Went to the Senior Bowl and combine.
- Was the first player drafted from UofL in the 2017 draft.

Dang, that's a story, right? But at times, that story never quite felt "enough" to me. God had blessed me in a way totally unimaginable, and He has with the NFL as well, but I'm telling you, there were seasons of my life where none of that was enough for me.

I was the only long snapper drafted in the 2017 NFL Draft. After being drafted, I thought maybe I'd play for ten plus years, pad up the bank account, help my wife go to school and live a cushy life. That was what my mindset had become.

I had trusted God, taken a Leap and He got me to where I thought I wanted to be. Then I decided it was time to take back the reins of my life. He set my future on a tee, and I only needed to drive it straight down the fairway . . . until a storm blew in. A brief phone call on the Saturday after training camp meant moving back home to live with my parents and start substitute teaching instead of setting up my new life in Pittsburgh. It doesn't take too long in this life to remember we're not in control.

If variety is the spice of life, God must have a keen palette, because He sure loves variety—not just from person to person or culture to culture, but for us as individuals. We experience our own variety all the time. I don't believe in coincidence only because I know He has specifically created you and I for a purpose.

Read that again because that reality doesn't always stick:

He has specifically created you and me for His purpose.

That's the million-dollar question. What's the point of my purpose on earth? As a Christian, your purpose should be pretty clear: to love others as Christ loved the church. Yet God created us all with different passions, fires that light us up—passions that should all be centered around His specific purpose. When we mix that up, the prayer changes from "God, please reveal to me how I can help advance your kingdom today" to "God, please help me achieve this goal that I have in life, because once I do that, I'll be in a better position to help you advance the kingdom."

How boring would life be if we all did the same thing. If every path was alike and we all experienced the same emotions and events. Like we were just a human conveyor belt. That's not how it is, obviously. So why do we constantly put ourselves in a box? A box that says "because I'm doing ____ right now, I'm meant to follow this path for the rest of my life."

That's a pretty big translation mix up from, "Take up your cross daily and follow me."

We're not being called to take just one Leap because there will be multiple times to pivot and jump again. For a season of my life, God has wanted to use football as a platform to introduce me to people, but that doesn't mean that is the same platform He will use throughout my life. That's the variety of life and the way God can use you—changing, evolving passions allow us to reach as many people as possible. For you to be able to relate to as many people as possible.

I referenced it earlier in the book, but focus on the way that Paul talks in Romans about the gifts that God gives us in Chapter 12:

"For just as each of us has one body with many members, and these members do not all have the same function, so in Christ we, though many, form one body, and each member belongs to all the others. We have different gifts, according to the grace given to each of us. If your gift is prophesying, then prophesy in accordance with your faith; if it is serving, then serve; if it is teaching, then teach; if it

is to encourage, then give encouragement; if it is giving, then give generously; if it is to lead, do it diligently; if it is to show mercy, do it cheerfully." —Romans 12:4-8

Each one of us is a different part of the body, but beyond that, all of our gifts, or passions, were given to us specifically, by the grace of God, to serve His body. Couple that with the way Jesus talks to his disciples about their role, about their gifts, or "spices."

Jesus talks to his disciples about salt, leading up to calling them (and us) to be salt of the earth. What good is salt if it loses its saltiness? It's not, there is no more use for it. God's not going to use you as salt just once, He's got a whole mess of spices waiting for you, they're not all the same, and they don't always follow the recipe that you're "supposed to" be on, but they all have a purpose. The first Leap is fantastic, and should help inspire you to continue Leaping, continue actively trusting God. Where is your identity? If you feel like you're falling instead of floating, maybe it's time to start looking for the next place to jump from.

Back in Chapter 11, I mentioned my friends, Clif Marshall and Shilo Becker. I gave a brief description on their roles in my life, but the following will dive into their Leap! It's a chance to fix the spotlight on two influential Leapers I know, and I hope you glean something from their stories as well. But there is a specific purpose in sharing their stories. It's to start to orient *your own* thinking in how God is calling you to Leap.

Once you read their stories and get into the right mindset, you're ready for this book's final call to action.

"MY LEAP!" BY CLIF MARSHALL

"Friendship is the hardest thing in the world to explain. It's not something you learn in school. But if you haven't learned the meaning of friendship, you really haven't learned anything." —*Muhammad Ali*

On December 16th, 2008, my wife and I fell to our knees by a wooden cross outside of a church in Florence, Kentucky. Broken and desperate. At that time, I was working in Cincinnati as a strength and conditioning coach.

I was 28-years-old. I finally knew what it meant to be born again. I had lived a reckless life from the time I was a teenager into my twenties. You see, my wife and I were high school sweethearts. We had reaped many years of bad decisions in our relationship that included lying, cheating, and alcohol abuse until we were forced to stop flirting with disaster and become born again by giving our life to Christ.

We saved our marriage and in return have been blessed with a great testimony: two beautiful children, and a great run as a strength and conditioning coach where I am currently sharing my story for God's glory in hopes it will impact athletes in a positive way. My wife and I are still flawed in many ways, but we share our testimony so that, through forgiveness, many other marriages will be saved. Satan wants to attack families by separation and it's our heart that we can save just one marriage through our story.

When I did run back to Christ in my life, it forced me to look at how I was coaching athletes.

This period of my career, around the year 2008, is where I experienced my truest Leap to date. I had been accustomed to the strength coaches who yell, belittle and curse their athletes in hopes it will make them "tough" and make the coach look tougher. God said to me "toughness" is loving your athletes and being vulnerable with them.

Early on in my coaching career, the goal was results-driven: bigger, faster, and stronger athletes with the quantitative data to prove it. That was an empty goal. I have learned that results are temporary, but relationships are eternal.

My aim is to not only strengthen athletes physically, but to also strengthen them mentally and spiritually. 1 Timothy 4:8 says "For physical training is of some value, but godliness has value for all things, holding promise for both the present life and the life to come." I now coach with an eternal perspective. Of the 400 professional athletes I have trained, God won't ask me how many of them bench pressed 300 pounds or how many ran a 40 yard dash in 4.3 seconds, or how many jumped 40 inches. He will simply ask me how I loved my athletes.

"MY LEAP!" BY SHILO BECKER

"Faith is to believe what you do not see; the reward of this faith is to see what you believe." —Saint Augustine

As the year 2020 progressed, there was talk of a so many things happening in the world: Locust invasion in Africa, killer wasps in Washington, the Philippines volcano eruption, the Turkey earthquake, Australia's bushfires, and Kobe (and Gianna) Bryant's plane crash and death, just to name a few. However, nothing prepared me or the world for what March 2020 had in store.

COVID-19 turned my life (and so many others) completely upside down and led me down a path of sadness, until my faith brought me back.

Once March came, we were warned of the dangers of COVID-19 and watched as the world slowly shut down. At the time, I was working for a hotel company and each day that passed was filled with so many questions—knowing that every shift that passed could be my last. March 15 was the last day I worked before I was put on a leave of absence. We were told that we'd return around June or July. As the months droned on, we were told of a possible extension and eventual layoffs—due to decreased demand in the hospitality industry.

On a summer day, I answered a phone call and was told that the position I held at the time was being terminated. My heart fell out of my chest and into my stomach. I wasn't given very many details—or maybe I was. To be quite honest, my memory for the day and phone call is foggy, genuinely not something I like to think about. It was at that moment I knew I had to update my resume and begin my search for a new job.

Little did I know, God was getting me ready for my Leap.

Days, weeks, and eventually months went by and I applied for so many jobs. I applied for everything I could find under the sun, whether or not I was qualified for the position or not. Rejection after rejection came in different formats: phone calls, emails and complete silence. Nothing prepared me for the hurt I was about to feel—rejection went back and forth from feeling everything to feeling nothing. However, nothing hurt more than being told I was overqualified for a job that I applied to.

I was willing to take a pay cut and work any hours or whatever else the role required.

Each rejection hurt more than the last, and eventually I gave up. Whenever the feeling of numbness returned, I would somehow come across a job that wanted to interview me: in-person and/

or online. Rejection became such a big part of each day in all of those months. My tears never seemed to dry nor end, and the puffiness from my eyes never seemed to subside.

I spent days on my couch and weeks in my bed, replaying the rejection conversations over and over. I went days without eating, and/or showering. I spent days in the dark: lights off and blinds closed. I decided enough was enough and reminded myself that things that are meant to be, will be. I decided to turn to my faith, to let go and let God. A few more days had passed, and I finally began to hear back from a couple of companies that were willing to hire me. As I took the interviews, their hourly wage, even as a full-time worker, unfortunately would not allow me to pay for half of my rent, let alone even half of my utilities. Something in me told me to not accept any of those jobs. I justified the decision and the feelings by thinking about how the wage wouldn't allow me to pay for any bills and would increase the risk of interacting with someone who had COVID. I cried every day, throughout the day, to the point where I was avoiding interactions of any sort: phone calls, text messages, Facetime calls, and even emails. I stopped applying for jobs. I couldn't take the rejection anymore; it was too painful. I had to remind myself, God has a plan.

Suddenly, I remembered John 3:17, "Jesus replied, 'You do not realize now what I am doing, but later you will understand." So as much as I could, I let go of my anger and my sadness. I left my bed and couch, I asked my significant other to take me out, which he happily obliged to. I refused to be still, in the same environment, harboring ill feelings. I opened the windows before we left, so that the negative energy would shift and leave. A few days later, I received a phone call for a company that I had applied to, for a front desk position.

The interview was scheduled, all I had to do now was wait. The wage they were offering was finally something more than minimum wage, not by much but still, enough to pay rent at the beginning of the month. Every morning after the phone call, up until the day of the interview, I spoke to God in my head, repeating the same mantra that I had been saying to myself for months: "if this is meant to be, it will be." The morning of, I sat down with myself and wrote out how much minimum of pay I would need to be able to afford my rent and wrote out beside it, how much the position I was going to interview for was offering and how much overtime I would need weekly, to make ends meet – and by making ends meet, I meant paying my necessary bills off, which did not include groceries and growing my savings account. I repeated John 3:17 to myself, "Jesus replied, 'You do not realize now what I am doing, but later you will understand."

Walking towards the building, I felt like someone was walking with me, and my nervousness died out. I suddenly felt warm, like I was being hugged, yet no one was near me. As I entered the double doors, things just felt right. A few days passed, and I started to doubt myself and feel sad again. John 3:17 crept back into my head. "Jesus replied, 'You do not realize now what I am doing, but later you will understand." Radio silence continued as a few more days had passed. Right when I believed that the interview didn't go as well as I thought, my phone rang. I ended up being offered a position that was higher than the one I had originally applied for, with pay that would allow all of my bills to be taken care of: including groceries and my savings account. Tears flooded out of my eyes and in that moment, I understood. I did not realize what God was doing, but now, I understood.

"MY LEAP!" BY (YOU)

"Do or do not. There is no try." —Yoda

Ideally, after reading this book, you have grown to realize that following Christ possesses a specific call to action. The Gospel aside, whether you are reading a book, listening to a sermon/podcast, or having a conversation with someone—the best interactions often end with a call to action.

When you heed that call to action, you are one step closer to self-evaluation and an important reminder: God has been faithful with your past, and he will be faithful with your future. So the call to action, for you, is coming shortly. But first, let me preface the CTA with the Truth in God's Word.

As much as I enjoyed writing this book and sharing a collection of stories and ideas, we *all* have a story to tell. It's not just me, or Shilo, or Clif, or Aaron Nance. Every single one of us has a unique story for a unique platform. Paul writes about this in his first letter to the church in Corinth.

There are different kinds of gifts, but the same Spirit distributes them. There are different kinds of service, but the same Lord. There

*are different kinds of working, but in all of them and in everyone it
is the same God at work. Now to each one the manifestation of the
Spirit is given for the common good. To one there is given through
the Spirit a message of wisdom, to another a message of knowledge
by means of the same Spirit, to another faith by the same Spirit, to
another gifts of healing by that one Spirit, to another miraculous
powers, to another prophecy, to another distinguishing between
spirits, to another speaking in different kinds of tongues, and
to still another the interpretation of tongues. All these are the
work of one and the same Spirit, and he distributes them to each
one, just as he determines." —1 Corinthians 12:4-11 (NIV)*

Now are you ready for a specific call to action?

*First, I urge you to read 1 Corinthians 12 in its entirety. Then, write
one of your stories.*

If you're like me (a visual learner), look up a picture or two from
the story you are writing about. Immerse yourself in the mind
frame you were in at that time. Reflect on how you got to your
moment when you Leapt off of the diving board or out of the
plane and let God take control.

I want to hear as many of these stories as possible. I want to
hear from as many people about how God changed your life and
when you allowed Him to work. There is something so beautiful and comforting reflecting on where God has led you, and the
gentle reminder in the words of Albert Tate, "God didn't take
you this far just to leave you here!".

LEAP!

Sit down, pray, reflect, write your story. Then step up onto a different kind of diving board. Move close to the edge, and share your Leap with others. Share your story with me!

If you're wondering who to share it with, I'd love to be the first person on that list. Write your story down, however long or short, edited or word vomited and share it on my website—a place where we can jump together.

A place for parakletos.

ACKNOWLEDGEMENT

I would like to spend a moment thanking and acknowledging everyone who has helped me on this journey—not only for the journey of this book, but who have shaped me throughout life in general.

It's an honor to thank my wife, Lauren, who in so many ways is my better half—making sacrifices, adding support and loving me more than I am able to even see. Throughout our marriage, you have been a constant reminder of what it means to trust and take a Leap in something that is outside of one's control!

I would like to thank Will Severns and Alex Demczak. You guys have helped me truly create something I didn't know was possible. The support, vision and coaching you gave, as well as encouragement, not only spurred me on to enthusiastically pursue this project, but to create something more from it. Your friendship is a blessing in both mine and Lauren's life.

To my parents and family. For supporting me from the diving board, to stadiums, last second trips to the airport, helping with our dog and constant other things that I don't thank you enough for. So much of my journey has had the spotlight on me, but there is no way this could have happened without you. From the aluminum bleachers down the road to freezing cold seats hours away, you guys were there—bringing a little bit of home to wherever we went.

The Morgan family. Chris, you and Tammy have had a greater impact on Lauren and I than you will ever know. I am so thankful for your faithful discipleship—not only to us, but for all of the souls that you have reached in your ministry. You changed the course of my life and I am forever thankful.

To everyone else who has had an impact on my life and on Lauren's life. In our family, our crazy adventures, from little league sports, to preparing for a baby. As iron sharpens irons, whether it be for 2 months or 20 years, I can't thank you enough for always supporting me on my wild adventures, and continually sharpening me.

Luke Combs sums up my emotions and gratitude with his song, *Without You*:

"It's me they love to give the credit to
But me don't mean a thing without you"

So oftentimes, because of my platform, I am the face that gets the credit, I get the attention and have the stories that people are curious about. I am truly beyond thankful for all of your love and support that have helped me have the courage, and faith to trust God, and take the Leaps that He has called me on.

ABOUT THE AUTHOR

Colin Holba

Colin and his beautiful wife, Lauren, live in Louisville, KY. They have one son, Roman, and a dog, Sheldon.

Share your Leap with Colin:

www.ColinHolba.com

Or shoot him a message today on social media:

@ColinHolba

PRAISE FOR AUTHOR

"One of my favorite phrases is 'Grow where you have been planted.' Colin Holba has consistently lived this out. From being a student manager on the UofL Baseball team, to walking on the UofL football, to earning a football scholarship, to being drafted in the NFL. Colin has made the most of every opportunity he has been given and he has not only grown but blossomed. It's been a joy to watch Colin succeed in many roles and I'm proud to call him a friend."

- CHRIS MORGAN, UNIVERSITY OF LOUISVILLE CHAPLAIN

"As a high school baseball coach, I was able to witness some of Holba's most endearing attributes: commitment, determination, passion & persistence. These characteristics, along with his endless appetite to learn. All have served him well throughout his career. Undeterred by life's inevitable challenges, I've seen Holba 'Leap' and land on solid ground time and again. It is my privilege to have been called "coach," but it is an honor to call Holba 'friend.'"

- RALPH GALI, FORMER VICE PRESIDENT OF ECOLAB

"Whatever Colin puts his heart to you can bet he'll succeed. He's the definition of a fighter, but also an amazing friend. Anyone who is interested in going after an insurmountable goal can learn from Colin's journey."

- JORDAN MATTHEWS, NFL WIDE RECEIVER

"Colin has a neat story to tell and is an inspiration to many. Seeing his journey go from a high school student athlete, to a college baseball manager, to an eventual NFL draft pick, to (my personal favorite) speaking to our team at a chapel service. I have seen what resilience, belief, faith, toughness and strength can do for one's path. Combine that with a love of Jesus Christ and it becomes clearer how true Leaps are possible."

- DAN MCDONNELL, UNIVERSITY OF LOUISVILLE HEAD BASEBALL COACH

"Colin I and became best friends right as he made it on to the University of Louisville football team as a walk-on. I had a front row seat to watch him put everything he had into his football dreams, and reap the benefits of those sacrifices. Off the field, I look up to him just as much. Colin practices what he preaches, and is not only a friend who is there for you when times are tough—he's willing to jump into that foxhole and conquer hard times with you. It's only fitting that the title of this book is Leap, because Colin is not just telling you to do so.

He's showing you how to, and is willing to do it right beside you as you take the Leap."

- WES BAKER, ESQUIRE

Made in the USA
Las Vegas, NV
07 August 2021